WOODWORK

Woodwork

E. J. WYNTER M.C.C.Ed.

HEAD OF THE BOYS' CRAFT DEPARTMENT
HAZELWICK COMPREHENSIVE SCHOOL, CRAWLEY, SUSSEX

All the illustrations are by the author

LONGMAN

LONGMAN GROUP LIMITED
London
*Associated companies, branches and representatives
throughout the world*

© Longman Group Ltd 1970
First published 1970
SBN 582 23391 7

Printed in Great Britain by
T. & A. Constable Ltd, Edinburgh.

Acknowledgements

We are grateful to the following for permission to reproduce copyright material:

Associated Lancashire Schools Examining Board for questions from 1966 C.S.E. Woodwork examination; British Standards Institution for extract from B.S. 1186, part I, 1952 and B.S. 565, 1963; Croid Ltd. for extracts from leaflets; East Anglian Examinations Board for questions from 1966 C.S.E. Woodwork examination; East Midland Regional Examinations Board for questions from 1966 C.S.E. Woodwork examination; English Abrasives Corporation Ltd. for Table 'A' from *Abrasives in Action*; Fibre Building Board Development Organisation Ltd. for an extract from charts and technical handbook; Formica International Ltd. for an extract from charts and booklet on laminated plastics; GKN Screws and Fasteners Ltd. for an extract from leaflet on screws and fasteners; T. S. Harrison & Sons Ltd. for extracts adapted from Union Jubilee and Union Graduate Woodturning Lathes leaflets; the Controller of Her Majesty's Stationery Office for extracts adapted from Forest Products Research Laboratories *Handbook of Hardwoods* and *Handbook of Softwoods*; Middlesex Regional Examining Board for questions from 1966 C.S.E. Woodwork Craft Knowledge examination; Norton Abrasives Ltd. for extracts from booklet *How to sharpen with India Oilstones*; Panad Publicity Services Ltd. for information on laminated plastics; William Ridgway & Sons Ltd. for extracts adapted from *Wood boring tools: Bits*; South-East Regional Examinations Board for questions from 1966 C.S.E. Woodwork examination; Southern Regional Examinations Board for questions from 1967 C.S.E. Woodwork examination; Spear & Jackson Ltd. for extracts from *Concerning Handsaws*; Stormont Archer Ltd. for extracts from their catalogue; Welsh Joint Education Committee for use of questions from 1966 C.S.E. Woodwork examination; West Midlands Examinations Board for questions from 1966 C.S.E. Woodwork examination.

Preface

The aim of this book is to provide a sound theoretical knowledge of the normal workshop practice found in most school woodcraft rooms. It includes the basic tools, materials, and processes and embraces the standard required by the various regional C.S.E. Examining Boards.

To enjoy the pleasure of creative work demands a reasonable proficiency with the tools and an understanding of the materials and processes of the craft. It is hoped that the following chapters will provide the necessary groundwork to enable boys to understand woodcraft and start them on lines of thought and enquiry leading to the designing and making of things giving lasting pleasure.

My thanks and appreciation to those colleagues who assisted me in my research, and in particular to Mr A. J. Chapman and Mr H. Jubb.

I would also like to mention my appreciation of the willing assistance I have had from the British Standards Institution, the various tool manufacturers and timber and materials merchants.

E. J. WYNTER 1970

Note on Metrication

Although the complete change to the metric system is expected to take many years, it is hoped that the major part will be completed by 1975.

Timber For some time to come hardwood will continue to be imported in Imperial measure. Equipment and labour in the hardwood producing countries do not make the change to metric units an easy operation, and because some of their best customers, the U.S.A. for instance, use Imperial measure they feel no urgency to make the change though the problems of metricating are being discussed.

Basic sawn sizes of softwood have been agreed together with basic lengths and the preparation allowances from the sawn size. These allowances vary according to the size of the timber and the class of work and would be confusing to the pupil at the bench. For this reason it has been suggested in this book that the preparation of a piece of timber by hand be standardised to the easily remembered 3 mm on the thickness, 6 mm on the width and 12 mm on the length.

The area of timber will be expressed in square metres.

Tools Plough planes are now being supplied with 4, 6, 9, and 12 mm cutters as standard equipment. Chisels are made to such a generous tolerance that many firms are simply marking them with the nearest metric size, though some firms are manufacturing chisels specially in the 12 mm and 18 mm sizes.

A leading manufacturer of bits has a thriving export order in inch units to all parts of the world, but does make one type of auger bit in metric sizes. Because of the high cost of making dies it may be some time before other varieties of bits are available in metric sizes.

Saws will be measured in millimetres and the method of specifying the spacing of the saw teeth will probably be discussed at an International Handtool Conference in 1971 or 1972. One saw manufacturer agrees that, meanwhile, we specify teeth points as so many per 25 mm.

No information is at present available about nails but wood screws have been given a low priority for discussion in view of the other more important problems which must be resolved. Woodscrews will continue to be made in inch sizes but should be known by their metric equivalent as set out in B.S.1210.

Although many decisions have yet to be made we in the craft room can make a start by thinking in metric units. This is best done by using completely metric rules and thinking of our timber as 50 by 25 instead of the usual 2 by 1. Once the habit of thinking in millimetres has been acquired there should be no difficulty in adjusting to the various recommendations which will appear from time to time.

INCHES	$\frac{3}{8}$	$\frac{1}{2}$	$\frac{5}{8}$	$\frac{3}{4}$	$\frac{7}{8}$	1	$1\frac{1}{4}$	$1\frac{1}{2}$	$1\frac{3}{4}$	2
MILLIMETRES	9.5	12.7	15.9	19.1	22.2	25.4	31.8	38.1	44.5	50.8

Metric Equivalents for Wood Screws. *From B.S.1210: 1963.*

Contents

Contents

I

Trees

Trees are the largest and oldest living things in the world, in fact some of the giant sequoias of California are over 360 feet high and more than 3000 years old.

From the earliest times, wood has been a great help to man. The caveman first burned wood to cook his food and keep him warm. He used wooden weapons to hunt animals and defend himself from enemies. Later, he made wooden tools and learned to build a hut and furnish it.

Today, wood plays an important part in modern industry, being used in building work as well as in the making of paper, rayon, and furniture. Many timbers have a delightful appearance and are valued for use in wall panelling and cabinet work. Wood is fairly light and reasonably strong, pleasant to touch and look at and can be cut, shaped, and joined quite easily. It can be fastened with glue, nails, and screws and finished in a variety of ways such as by painting or polishing.

Different timbers vary in many ways such as in weight, colour, durability, grain, and strength. Ash, for example, is tough and elastic, making it ideal for diving boards and other sports equipment. Greenheart is valued for fishing rods because it is very flexible, while teak, being acid resistant, is used for bench tops in science laboratories. Whatever the job, there is a suitable timber for it somewhere in the wide range from lightweight balsa to heavy lignum vitae.

Classification of Timbers

Timbers for woodwork use fall into two main classes:

(a) Softwoods

(b) Hardwoods

SOFTWOODS

These are timbers from trees such as the pine, fir, spruce, and larch, Fig. 1. They are known as conifers because their seeds are enclosed in cones. These trees have long needle like green leaves each of which lives four or five years. Because they are replaced a few at a time the trees always appear green and are often called 'evergreens', though larch is an exception. The structure of a softwood is simple and the wood is usually resinous, soft, and easy to work although some softwoods, such as yew, are quite hard.

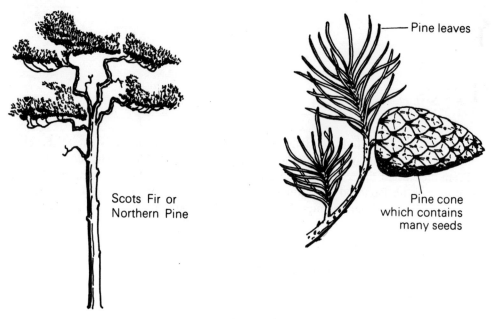

Fig. 1   A softwood

Conifers are found in the temperate zones and on mountain slopes.

HARDWOODS

These come from trees which have broad leaves such as the oak, ash, beech, and mahogany and are to be found in the warmer regions of the temperate zones and the tropics, Fig. 2. They are known as deciduous trees because they shed their leaves in the autumn. This prevents loss of water through their leaves in the winter when their roots are unable to absorb moisture from the cold ground. The seeds of deciduous trees are enclosed in fruits.

The structure of a hardwood is complex and the timber usually hard and a little difficult to work, but some hardwoods such as balsa and willow are quite soft. The terms 'hardwood' and 'softwood' for timber classification date back to the days of the village carpenter whose experience was limited to a few locally grown timbers.

Softwood is in great demand for building work such as roofs, staircases, floors, and general constructional work, and is used in much greater quantities than the harder, heavier, and more expensive hardwoods which are normally used for high class interior joinery work and furniture making.

THE MAIN PARTS OF A TREE

A tree consists of five main parts:

Oak in Summer   Oak in Winter

Fig. 2   A hardwood

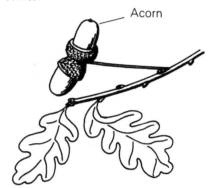

The acorn is the fruit of the oak.
In each acorn is one seed

1. *Roots*. These search for various mineral salts in the moist ground. They also hold the tree firmly in place during storms.
2. *Trunk*. This part acts as a support for the branches which it raises as high as possible towards the light. It is from the trunk that we get our timber.
3. *Branches*. By forming as many branches as possible the tree develops a large crown of leaves.
4. *Leaves*. These manufacture food for the tree through the action of sunlight and air.
5. *Bark*. The bark protects the growing part of the tree from the weather and animals.

HOW A TREE GROWS, Fig. 3

In the spring, the warm sunshine evaporates the moisture in the leaves. This causes a watery solution of mineral salts to be absorbed by the roots and flow through the sap-wood of the trunk and branches to the leaves. This watery solution is called sap. The action of the sunlight and air now turns these mineral salts in the leaves into a food of sugar and starch which then flows down through the inner bark, or bast, to feed every part of the tree. On the way down much of this food is absorbed by the rays which are horizontal radial cells scattered throughout the tree. These rays, once known as medul-lary rays, are food storage cells.

CAMBIUM

This is the actual living part of the tree and consists of a complete film all over between the bark and the wood. On the inner side of the cambium grow the new wood cells while

3

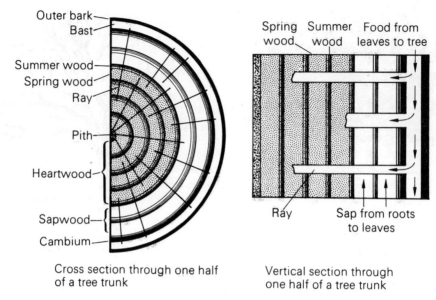

Cross section through one half
of a tree trunk

Vertical section through
one half of a tree trunk

Fig. 3   Growth of a tree

on the outer side grow the new cells to form bast. If a piece of bark is removed from a growing tree in the springtime a slimy film will be seen. This is the cambium layer. The position of this layer explains why we often find living trees which are hollow shells, the centre part having rotted away or been eaten by insects.

SAPWOOD, Fig. 3

This is the active part of the tree. It is usually pale in colour and can be clearly seen in most planed timbers. Because these cells contain food and water most sapwood is usually attacked by fungi or eaten by insects unless it is treated with preservative such as creosote. In sapwood, all the cells are open to each other and this allows the liquid preservative to soak right in.

B.S.1186, Part 1:1952, states that sound sapwood is permissible in joinery work except where the work has to be stained. It adds that sapwood is acceptable for interior joinery only, but must be treated with preservative against attack by the lyctus beetle. The only exceptions are beech and birch which are not affected by this insect.

HEARTWOOD

After several years the wood in the middle is unable to play an active part in the life of the growing tree because it is too far from the cambium layer. When this happens the food in the cells is absorbed into the cell walls which thicken and harden. Chemical changes now take place, the cells seal themselves off from each other and this part of the tree dies. This dead part, called the heartwood, now only serves as a strong framework or

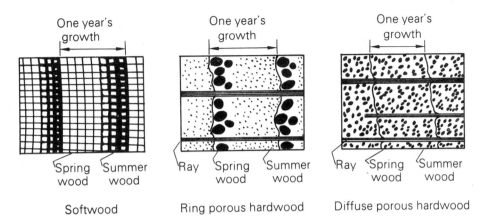

One year's growth

Spring wood   Summer wood

Softwood

Ray   Spring wood   Summer wood

Ring porous hardwood

Ray   Spring wood   Summer wood

Diffuse porous hardwood

Fig. 4   Annual rings

skeleton to support the tree. As the years go by and more coatings of sapwood are formed, inner rings of sapwood die to form more heartwood.

It must not be imagined that because the heartwood is dead it is in a state of decay. Being dead simply means that it plays no further part in the life of the tree. The heartwood is the part most valued for woodwork.

Heartwood usually has a darker colour than sapwood. For this reason, in cabinet work, timber containing sapwood should be avoided because it spoils the appearance of the finished article besides being liable to woodworm attack.

GROWTH RING OF SOFTWOOD, Fig. 4

Wood consists of millions of cells packed tightly together from the roots to the leaves. In the spring the cambium makes many wide cells with thin walls to allow a large volume of sap to quickly reach the leaves. Because of the thin walls this wood appears pale and is soft and weak. In the summer the demand for sap is less and so the cambium makes narrower cells with thick walls. This wood appears dark in colour and is hard and strong and gives strength to the tree. During the winter the tree is at rest and there is no sap flow. Every year this cycle is repeated, the tree covering itself just behind the bark with a new layer of pale springwood followed by dark summerwood. If we examine the section of a tree trunk we can see these growth rings and by counting them we can tell the age of the tree. Being formed every year they are often known as annual rings.

GROWTH RINGS IN HARDWOODS, Fig. 4

Hardwood trees have large tubular cells for conducting the enormous quantity of sap required by the broad leaves. These large cells are called vessels and are many feet long. Wood fibres grow in a solid tight mass between the vessels to give strength to the tree. If the end grain of a piece of hardwood is examined the vessels are seen in cross-section and appear as holes, and when seen like this they are generally called pores.

In some trees, such as oak and ash, large vessels are formed in the spring and small vessels in the summer so the end grain shows distinct rings of large and small pores. Such woods are said to be RING POROUS. In other hardwoods, such as beech and mahogany, the vessels formed in the spring and summer are the same size throughout so that the end grain shows an even pattern of pores. These woods are said to be DIFFUSE POROUS.

In hardwoods, the growth rings are sometimes difficult to see, also the growth does not take place regularly each year. For this reason the name growth rings is more accurate than annual rings.

Exercises

1. For commercial use, timbers are classified into two types. State what these two types are and why they are so called.

2. Name the five main parts of a tree.

3. What is the difference between heart and heartwood?

4. What are rays? In which group of timbers would you expect to clearly see them?

5. Draw the end-view of a hardwood log. Make the drawing about three inches across. Label the following features:

   (i)   Growth ring

   (ii) Heartwood

   (iii) Sapwood

   (iv) Cambium

   (v)   Medullary rays

   Write a short paragraph on each explaining:

   (a) Its importance in the life of the tree.

   (b) How this information is of practical use.

   (ASSOCIATED LANCASHIRE SCHOOLS EXAMINING BOARD)

2

Conversion

The Conversion of Timber

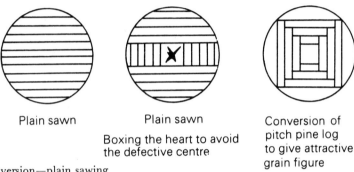

Plain sawn

Plain sawn
Boxing the heart to avoid
the defective centre

Conversion of
pitch pine log
to give attractive
grain figure

Fig. 5   Conversion—plain sawing

Although a tree is felled in winter when the sap is at rest, more than one half of its weight consists of water. After felling, the tree is sawn or converted into lengths of convenient size so that it can be more easily dried. The simplest way of converting a log is to saw it into parallel boards. This is called 'plain', 'through and through', or 'flat' sawing and is a quick and cheap method of conversion, Fig. 5.

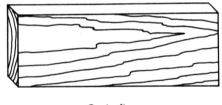

Grain figure

When plain sawn, the outer boards have poor wearing qualities and may warp badly in shrinking. In a number of hardwoods this method also results in the outer boards having an uninteresting appearance. A better method of conversion is to have the log quarter sawn. That is, the log is quartered and all cuts are kept radially on the line of the rays as far as possible, Fig. 6. This method of conversion produces hard wearing surfaces suitable for flooring, and boards free from warping, because the shrinking is even. In hardwoods, quarter sawing exposes the rays along their length which may form an attractive pattern known as 'silver grain', or figure. This increases the value of the wood which is in great demand for cabinet work and panelling.

Quarter sawing requires expert handling of the log on the sawing table and can waste

7

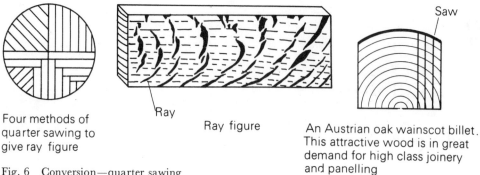

Four methods of
quarter sawing to
give ray figure

Ray figure

Ray

An Austrian oak wainscot billet.
This attractive wood is in great
demand for high class joinery
and panelling

Fig. 6   Conversion—quarter sawing

a lot of timber, consequently the quarter sawn wood is more expensive than plain sawn.
If stability, hard wearing qualities, or appearance is important then the extra cost is well
repaid.

Seasoning

This is the period during which the excess water in green timber is removed by a natural
or an artificial process. Unseasoned timber is too difficult to cut properly and accurate
work is impossible due to the gradual change in the size and shape of the wood as it
shrinks in drying out. Also, being wet, the surface cannot be painted or polished and
there is a constant risk of mould and fungi attack.

There are several methods of seasoning but the two most general are:
(a) Air seasoning
(b) Kiln seasoning

AIR SEASONING, Fig. 7

The boards are neatly stacked and
separated from each other by 25 mm
square strips of clean softwood called
stickers. These are placed at regular
intervals along the boards and vertically
in line. The stack is built on brick legs at
least 450 mm tall on a ground of concrete
or cinders to prevent any risk of disease
from grass or weeds attacking the wet
timber. The whole area is well ventilated
and the only cover is a roof to give protection from the sun and rain. Evaporation
takes place naturally with the free circulation of air between the boards and round

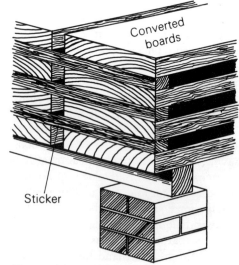

Converted
boards

Sticker

Fig. 7   Air seasoning

8

the stack and it is usual to allow 1 year's seasoning for every 25 mm thickness of the timber.

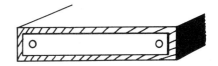

Fig. 8 Thin metal cleats nailed to the ends of boards slow down the rate of drying

The ends of the boards tend to dry out too rapidly and this causes splitting. To slow down this drying the ends are sealed with waterproof paint or covered with thin strips of metal, called cleats, nailed in position, Fig. 8. Wooden cleats should not be used becuase they cannot bend when the wood shrinks.

KILN SEASONING, Fig. 9

The timber is stacked on a truck exactly as for air seasoning then wheeled into the kiln and the doors closed. Warm moist air is blown through the stack of timber and this evaporates the water from inside the boards while keeping the outside damp. If this were not done the outside would dry out quickly and the surface of the boards would set hard. This is called case hardening, Fig. 10. Further heating would then make the interior develop a great number of cracks as it tried to shrink. This is known as honeycombing and weakens the timber as well as spoiling its appearance when re-sawn. Warm air is used because it holds more moisture than cold air. Heat is supplied by radiators, the air is moistened by steam jets and circulation made by fans. After a while the moisture in the air is reduced and the heat gradually increased until the timber is seasoned. The whole process takes from $1\frac{1}{2}$ to 6 weeks depending on the type of wood being seasoned.

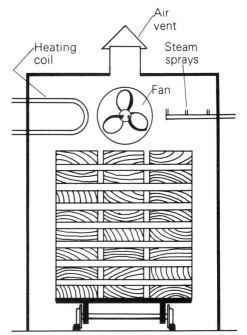

Fig. 9   Kiln seasoning

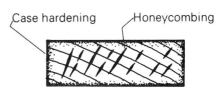

Fig. 10

Air and kiln seasoning are often used together, but there is still a lot of prejudice against kiln seasoning just as there is against most new methods when first used. The following facts are worth considering:

Air seasoning:
1. Takes a long time.
2. Takes up a lot of space.
3. There is always a risk of insect and fungi attack.
4. Some woods, e.g., oak, are difficult to air season because they split.
5. The moisture content can only be reduced to about 17 per cent.
6. The method is cheap.
7. No special skill is required.

Kiln seasoning:
1. Takes a short time.
2. Any insects' eggs in the timber are killed.
3. Moisture content is under control.
4. Great skill and care is required to produce sound timber.
5. This method is essential for timbers which have to be drier than normal for use in centrally heated buildings.
6. The equipment is expensive.
7. Low moisture content timber must have a ready sale otherwise if kept in the timber yard it will absorb moisture to the level of its surroundings.

In drying, the wood shrinks very little along its length, slightly across its diameter, but quite a lot round the circumference following the growth rings. This makes the growth rings shorten in length which is why the outer boards of a log are pulled hollow or warp, Fig. 11.

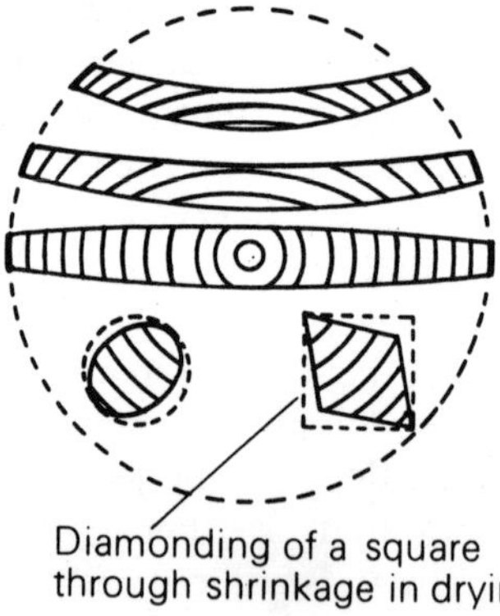

Eighteen per cent of the oven-dry weight of air seasoned timber is water, but this varies according to the moisture content or humidity of the air. Because of seasonal changes in the weather, wood must be allowed to expand and contract or it will split. Painting and polishing wood do not prevent this change in moisture content, but they do slow it down so that movement of the timber is reduced.

Diamonding of a square through shrinkage in drying

Fig. 11 Shrinking and warping. In drying, each annual ring shrinks along its circumference. This makes the outer boards curl and the centre board thinner at the two edges

For centrally heated offices and buildings, where the humidity is below the normal level, all furniture and joinery work must be made from timber with a moisture content of about 12 per cent, Fig. 12. To get timber as dry as this the kiln must be used.

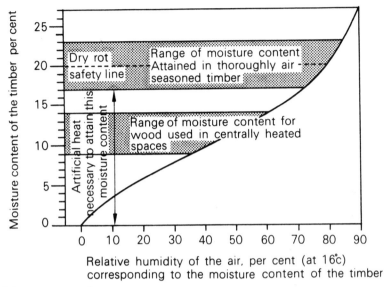

Fig. 12   Moisture content chart

Defects

RESIN POCKET

A resin filled gap found in softwoods. The resin flows round an injury to the tree to heal it and this results in a pocket or gap being formed in the wood.

KNOT, Fig. 13

Part of a branch enclosed in the wood by the natural growth of the tree. A sound, tight

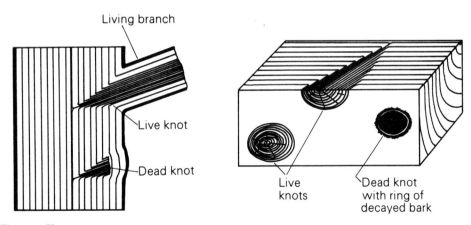

Fig. 13   Knots

11

knot, also known as a live knot, results from a branch in actual growth at the time the tree was felled. These knots are harder than the surrounding wood and light orange in colour. A dead knot is dark coloured and results from a branch which died long before the tree was felled. There is usually a black line of decay round the edge and the knot may be loose and fall out to leave a knot hole. Knots are named after their shape.

Boards containing many knots are unsuitable for flooring because the softer wood wears away leaving the harder knots in the form of bumps. Instead, knotty wood is used as a decorative wall covering, especially in Canada and America.

SHAKES, Fig. 14

These are large cracks in the log and follow the two directions of weakness in the timber: (a) between the growth rings and (b) along the rays. Small shakes are often called checks. These faults occur in the growing tree, at the time of felling and during seasoning.

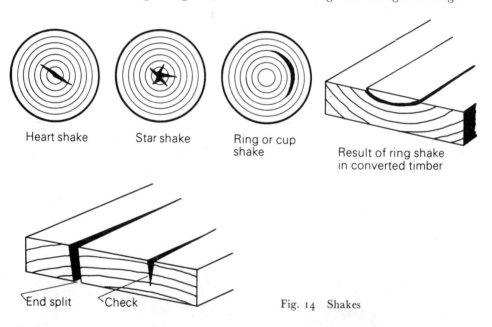

Heart shake Star shake Ring or cup shake Result of ring shake in converted timber

End split Check

Fig. 14 Shakes

CUPPING, BOWING, SPRINGING, AND TWISTING

These defects result from seasoning faults and difficulties caused by the tree not growing straight, Fig. 15.

WANE OR WANEY EDGE, Fig. 16

This is the edge of a piece of wood which includes the outside of the tree. Bark may still be on the edge which, of course, is sapwood. Waney elm boards are often used in the making of garden furniture and for covering the sides of sheds.

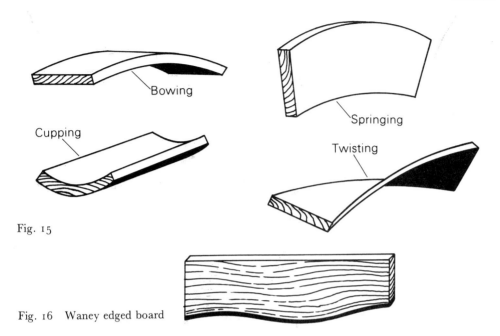

Fig. 15

Fig. 16   Waney edged board

Diseases

Timber left in a damp, badly ventilated place will soon be attacked and destroyed by fungi, the spores of which are always floating in the air. To prevent this disaster the moisture content of timber must be kept below 20 per cent, by storing and using it in a well ventilated place.

DRY ROT

This is the worst of these diseases because the fungus causing it spreads rapidly by means of fine thread like feelers which reach for all the wood in the vicinity. Soon the wood is turned into dry brown cubes which crumble to dust when handled.

INSECTS

In this country four kinds of insects cause considerable damage to wood. They are: pinhole borers, powder post beetle, furniture beetle, and the death watch beetle. Eggs are laid in cracks on the wood surface and the grubs eat their way through the wood to emerge some time later fully grown and ready to fly away. More eggs are laid and the tunnelling is repeated so that the wood eventually becomes riddled with holes and weakened.

Although the worm holes are the exit holes of the pest, if the timber is serving some important purpose such as part of a roof, careful spraying and treatment by experts can often save the timber from further destruction.

13

Veneer

A veneer is a thin sheet of wood produced by:
(a) Rotary cutting — producing plain veneers for plywood
(b) Flat slicing ⎫
(c) Half rounding ⎬ producing decorative veneers for cabinet work
(d) Sawing ⎭

   In the first three methods the veneer is cut with a knife and there is no waste. Sawn veneers are thicker and there is a lot of waste so this rare method is only used for unusual timbers.

   The log must first be steamed in a tank for several days to make it soft and pliable. For rotary cutting, the whole log is mounted in a machine like a big lathe and rotated against a knife blade which moves slowly into the log so that the wood is peeled off in one continuous sheet, Fig. 17. This method generally produces a plain looking veneer suitable for the manufacture of plywood.

   Decorative veneers are highly valued in cabinet work because of their attractive appearance. The log is first sawn into flitches in the way which will produce the most attractive surfaces. In flat slicing, the veneer is sliced off in straight sheets by a long knife, Fig. 18. Some timbers produce their best veneers when 'half-rounded'. For this, the flitch is bolted to a frame which rotates the wood against the knife, Fig. 19.

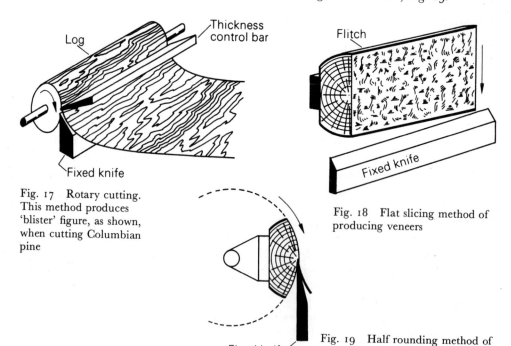

Fig. 17   Rotary cutting. This method produces 'blister' figure, as shown, when cutting Columbian pine

Fig. 18   Flat slicing method of producing veneers

Fig. 19   Half rounding method of producing veneers

Plywood, Fig. 20

A built-up sheet of wood made by gluing together an odd number of veneers or plies each having its grain direction at right-angles to the next. This results in a rigid sheet of wood which will not shrink, swell, or warp. An odd number of plies is used so that the grain on the outer faces runs in the same direction. The number of plies varies from 3 to 9 forming plywood sheets from 3 mm to 25 mm thick. Sheet sizes range from 1 500 mm by 1 500 mm to 3 000 mm by 1 800 mm, the first dimension denoting the direction of the grain on the faces.

Alder, birch, beech, pine, and fir are commonly used for plywood manufacture though these may be faced with a veneer of oak, mahogany, or other choice hardwood for better appearance.

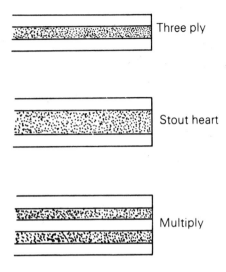

Fig. 20   Plywood

Originally, plywood was manufactured for the making of cheap boxes. Dampness caused the glue to soften and the plies came apart. This resulted in the product being regarded with contempt and for a long time no cabinet maker would use plywood. With the use of new and improved glues, plywood is now made to withstand the worst conditions and it is quite common today to use plywood for the hulls of sailing boats.

The gluing of the plies is called bonding and is graded as follows:

WBP   Weather and boil proof
BR   Boil resistant
MR   Moisture resistant
INT   For interior use

LAMINBOARD, Fig. 21

A built-up board consisting of a core of softwood strips not exceeding 7.1 mm in width. These strips are glued together and faced each side with a lamin or sheet of ply. The strips are arranged with their heart side on opposite sides to counteract warping, but being narrow there is very little movement.

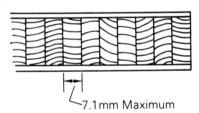

Fig. 21   Laminboard

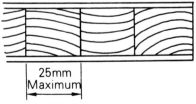

Fig. 22   Blockboard

BLOCKBOARD, Fig. 22

This is similar to laminboard except that the core is built up of softwood strips not exceeding 25 mm wide. Being wider there is more risk of the core strips warping.

Both laminboard and blockboard can be obtained with a thin veneer of decorative wood on both sides for use when the timber is to be seen as in cabinet work. The edges are then usually lipped with a hardwood strip to conceal the core.

The boards are available in several thicknesses from 13 mm upwards, but the two most popular sizes are 13 mm and 19 mm.

CHIPBOARD

This is made from wood chips bonded together with a resin glue under great pressure. The finished boards measure 2 400 mm by 1 200 mm by 12 mm and 19 mm thick. There are no grain problems as with natural timber and it is often used as a ground for decorative veneers.

HARDBOARD

This useful material is manufactured from wood fibres which are pulped, processed, and refined, then subjected to great pressure at high temperature. This results in a dense tough board with a perfectly smooth face on one side and a fine mesh pattern on the back. Hardboard is completely dry when it comes from the press and must be treated in a steam room to restore it to the moisture content of its surroundings. Hardboard differs from other manufactured boards in that the bond mainly results from the felting of the fibres and their own adhesive properties.

Before fixing hardboard to its framework it must be conditioned by damping it on the mesh side with ½ litre (1 pint) of water for a 2 438 mm by 1 219 mm (8 feet by 4 feet) board. It should be left for at least 24 hours and then fixed with rust-resisting nails. Failure to condition the board will cause it to swell and buckle after fixing.

DECORATIVE LAMINATED PLASTICS, Fig. 23

Laminated means consisting of a number of thin layers. These decorative laminates, such as Formica and Warerite, are made by assembling a large number of resin soaked paper sheets to form the base. A resin soaked decorative paper is placed on top and over this is laid a melamine resin treated skin which provides the tough surface. This sandwich is then placed between highly polished stainless steel sheets and pressed at high temperature for a carefully controlled period of time to complete the process.

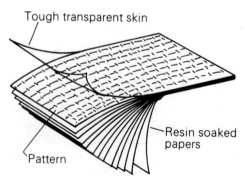

Fig. 23   Laminated plastic

Decorative laminates are hard wearing, clean looking, smooth, and attractive. They are made in a wide variety of patterns in sheets as large as 3 600 mm by 1 500 mm by 1·5 mm thick.

For fixing, synthetic resin adhesives are economical and reliable and give the worker time to position the sheet in place, but impact adhesives could be used if preferred.

Exercises

1. Name two important seasoning methods. State the advantages and disadvantages of each.

2. What is: (a) a live knot, (b) a dead knot, (c) a shake, (d) a split?

3. Make a neat sketch to show what is meant by: (a) cupping, (b) twisting, (c) bowing, (d) springing, (e) wane.

4. What is veneer?

5. Why is plywood made having an odd number of sheets?

6. How must hardboard be prepared before fixing it to a frame? Why must this be done? What kind of nails should be used?

7. *Either:*
   (a) Explain why wood cut from a newly felled tree is unsuitable for cabinet making. Briefly describe, in order, the essential things that happen to the timber from the time of felling in order to render it fit for use at the bench.
   Or:
   (b) Describe briefly what is meant by conversion. State what methods of conversion would be best for timber required for the following purposes:
   (i)   packing cases,
   (ii) to show annual ring figuring,
   (iii) to show medullary ray figuring.
   (MIDDLESEX REGIONAL EXAMINING BOARD)

8. Draw a circle approximately 75 mm in diameter. Then draw in this circle the cross-sections to show two methods of converting an oak log to provide the maximum number of figured boards.
   (SOUTH-EAST REGIONAL EXAMINATIONS BOARD)

9. Show the difference between plywood and blockboard and give an example of the use of each. When is it better to use plywood, and when is blockboard the more suitable material to use?
   (EAST ANGLIAN REGIONAL EXAMINATIONS BOARD)

3

Timber

A log is converted in two stages:

1. *Breaking down:* to saw it into a number of convenient sized pieces.

2. *Re-sawing:* to saw the convenient sized pieces to finished sizes.

Converted timber is known by the size and shape of its cross-section, the more common being board and strip, Fig. 24.

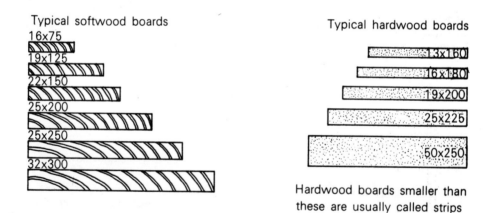

Typical softwood boards
16x75
19x125
22x150
25x200
25x250
32x300

Typical hardwood boards
13x160
16x180
19x200
25x225
50x250

Hardwood boards smaller than these are usually called strips

Fig. 24

Ordering Timber

The width and thickness of all timber is known by the size to which it is sawn in the timber yard. Boards are sold by the square metre which means the area of the board's surface in square metres regardless of the thickness. To find the area simply multiply the length of the board in metres by the width in millimetres and divide by 1 000.

$$\text{i.e. Length (m)} \times \frac{\text{Width (mm)}}{1\ 000} = \text{Area in sq. metres.}$$

Thus, a board 3 m long by 200 mm wide is 0.6 m² in area and a board 2.1 m long by 150 mm wide is 0.315 m² in area. The timber merchant's price list will show the price per square metre for each thickness of board.

The surface of sawn timber is rough, but for a small extra charge the timber merchant will plane it on his planing machine. This may be necessary if the wood is hard and there is a lot of it. Boards can be machine planed on both sides (P.B.S.), but strip and square can be planed all round (P.A.R.).

Although planing reduces the width and thickness of the timber it is still known by its sawn size. For this reason, after timber has been planed, the sawn size is called the nominal size because it is now the size of the timber in name only. A piece of sawn wood measuring 50 mm by 25 mm and planed all round to 47 mm by 22 mm would always be known as '50 by 25'.

Narrow stuff, such as strip and scantling, is sold by length in metres.

Having designed a piece of work and made a detailed drawing, a list of all the parts should be made showing the length, width, and thickness of each. These will be the finished sizes. To get each part straight, true, and smooth we must begin with bigger wood to allow for planing true. For bench work, the planing allowance on a board is:

3 mm extra on the thickness

6 mm extra on the width

12 mm extra on the length

The planing allowance on square stuff is:

3 mm extra on each side

12 mm extra on the length

Where a mortice is chopped out near the end of a leg, 25 mm extra on the length is a safer allowance to avoid the end grain splitting out.

The following table shows how a cutting list could be made out. It shows the parts, number required, and the finished size of each. The last column lists the size of the timber required to make the parts, that is with the planing allowance added.

CUTTING LIST

PART	NO. OFF	PLANED L W T	SAWN L W T
Legs	4	375 × 47 × 22	400 × 50 × 25
Long rails	2	425 × 72 × 22	437 × 75 × 25
Short rails	2	200 × 72 × 22	212 × 75 × 25
Top	1	460 × 230 × 16	472 × 236 × 19

Preparation of Timber to Size

1. Examine the timber all over, then select the better side.
2. Test it for winding, Fig. 25 (see chapter 5).
3. Plane it true and smooth. Take off as little wood as possible.
4. Test with a rule, Fig. 26:
   (a) Length
   (b) Width
   (c) Diagonals
5. When the wood is flat and true mark it with a pencil. This is called the FACE SIDE MARK and should point to the better edge.
6. Plane the better edge straight and square to the face side. Take off as little wood as possible.
7. Test with a rule and try square from the face side, Fig. 27.
8. When straight and square to the face side, mark with a pencil. This mark is called the FACE EDGE MARK and should point to the face side.
9. Set the marking gauge to width plus 0.5 mm inch for final cleaning with the smoothing plane.
10. Gauge all round from the face edge, Fig. 28.
11. Plane to the gauge line.
12. Set the marking gauge to the thickness plus 0.5 mm.
13. Gauge all round from the face side.
14. Plane to the gauge line.
15. Measure in 6 mm from one end.
16. Square a line all round. Use the try square against the face side and face edge and cut the line with a marking knife.
17. Saw off the waste wood, Fig. 29.
18. Measure to length.
19. Square a line all round using marking knife and try square.
20. Saw off the waste wood.

The wood is now to the correct length, width, and thickness and can be cleaned up

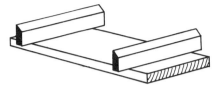

A Test for winding

B Plane better side

Fig. 25

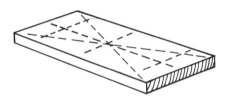

C Test in six positions, using a rule

D With a pencil, make the face side mark

Fig. 26

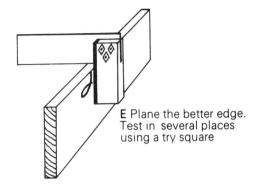

E Plane the better edge. Test in several places using a try square

F With a pencil, make the face edge mark

Fig. 27

G Gauge and plane to width, then gauge and plane to thickness

H Square the ends to length

Fig. 28

21

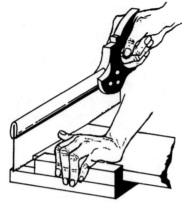

I Saw off the wastewood. Note the use of the left thumb to guide the saw

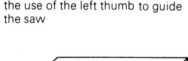

J The prepared wood

with a smoothing plane when required. All the faces are flat and true with the edges square to them. All wood must be brought to size like this so remember the planing order:

1. FACE SIDE
2. FACE EDGE
3. WIDTH
4. THICKNESS

All gauging must be done from the face side and the face edge. This prevents any error in the marking out, avoids confusion when working with several pieces of wood and ensures that the work will be correct when assembled.

Fig. 29

Exercises

1. What are the following:
   (a) board; (b) strip; (c) scantling?

2. By what measurement are boards sold?

3. To what size does the width and thickness of a board refer?

4. What is meant by the nominal size?

5. By what measurement is strip sold?

6. What is meant by the planing allowance on a piece of wood? State this allowance for bench work.

7. State the four main steps when preparing a piece of timber to size.

8. What is the purpose of the 'face side' and 'face edge' marks?

4

Safety and Handling

Safety Rules

There are many sharp tools in the woodwork room. This is good because they will cut wood so that you can make things, but to make sure that they do not cut you, learn the following rules:

1. Remove your jacket and roll up your sleeves.
2. Wear an apron.
3. Remove your tie.
4. Walk about the craft room — never run.
5. Carry tools pointing down and close to your side.
6. Keep both hands behind the cutting edge of tools.
7. When finished with a tool, return it to its place. A bench top covered with tools is dangerous. Heavy tools may fall on your feet, and sharp edges get knocked and broken.
8. If you are not sure, ask your teacher. It is dangerous to experiment with sharp tools and machines.
9. Do not touch any lever or switch on any machine unless you have been taught how to use it properly, understand its use, and have permission to use it.
10. Listen to your teacher and willingly do as you are asked. Remember, your teacher is there to help you.

Bench

This must be strong and rigid. The legs and framework should be made from 75 mm square deal and the bench top of beech at least 50 mm thick. The space along the centre of the bench top is the well and is used for the safe storage of tools. The bottom of the well can be of deal for economy. A suitable height for the bench top is not quite half the height of the worker.

BENCH STOP, Fig. 30

Use: To hold the timber when planing.

The bench stop is made of beech and placed at the left-hand end of the bench top.

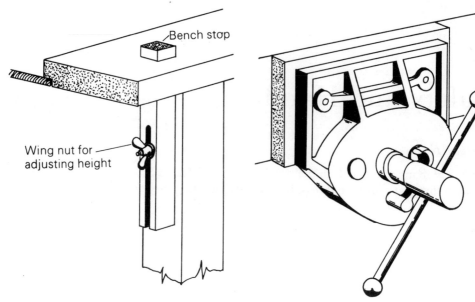

Fig. 30   Bench stop

Fig. 31   Bench vice

BENCH VICE, Fig. 31

Use. For gripping work.

Parts. 1. Body: Cast iron
          2. Sliding jaw: Cast iron
          3. Handle: Steel
          4. Screwed spindle: Steel
          5. Guides.   Steel

The bench vice is sometimes described as an extra pair of hands. The size is the width of the jaws, a suitable size being 229 mm, which opens out to 330 mm. Vices can be obtained having a quick release mechanism for rapid opening and closing.

The main body of the vice should be fixed to the underside of the bench and with the jaw face let into the side. Both jaws are then faced with beech to protect the work and tools.

BENCH HOOK, Fig. 32

Use. For holding timber when sawing across the grain.

The bench hook is also known as a sawing board. In use, the bottom batten hooks against the side of the bench, though it is often better to grip it in the vice, and the work is held against the top batten. When the wood is sawn through, the flat base of the bench hook supports the work and prevents splintering at the end of the cut.

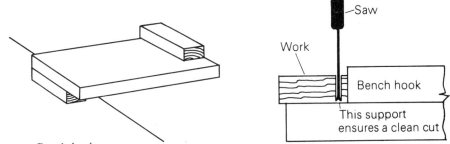

Fig. 32   Bench hook

SHOOTING BOARD, ALSO SHUTING BOARD, Fig. 33

Use. For the planing of narrow ends and edges. When we plane narrow edges we say

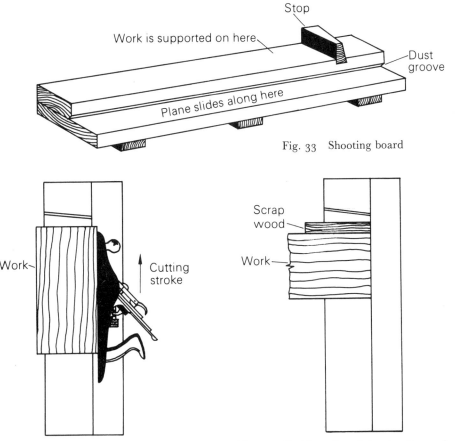

Fig. 33   Shooting board

Fig. 34   Shooting with the grain

Fig. 35   Position of work for shooting end grain

we are shooting them. It is difficult to shoot thin wood when held in the vice because the plane wobbles about. The work is made much easier if a shooting board is used.

To plane a thin edge the wood is held on the shooting board against the stop and over-hanging the side by 6 mm. To get a square edge to the timber the plane blade must be ground and sharpened straight, set fine, and the plane moved back and forth along the middle part of the work until no more shavings can be removed. Two or three shavings should then be taken off the whole length, Fig. 34.

To plane end grain, a piece of scrap wood is placed behind the work to prevent the end grain of the work from splitting. The plane must be pressed into the corner of the shooting board and worked back and forth while the wood is fed against the blade, Fig. 35.

A 600 mm shooting board is a handy size. In use it rests against the bench stop but a better method is to fix a length of wood to the base so that it can be held in the vice.

CRADLE, Fig. 36

Use. For supporting a length of square timber when planing off its corners.

This device can be quickly and easily made when the need arises, and is used against a bench stop or held in the vice.

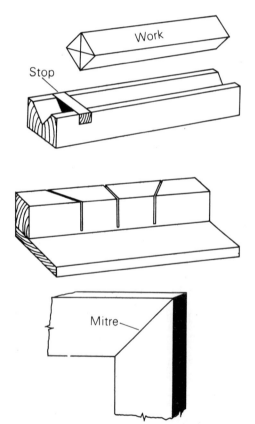

Fig. 36   Cradle: for holding a length of wood along a corner

MITRE BLOCK, Fig. 37

Use. To enable lengths of small section wood to be accurately mitred, that is, sawn at an angle of 45 degrees.

The mitre block is built up from two pieces of beech and has three saw cuts in the top piece; a 45-degree cut to the left and right and a 90-degree cut in the centre.

The 90-degree cut enables small stuff to be accurately sawn square.

Fig. 37   Mitre block

26

MITRE BOX, Fig. 38

Use. To enable large sections of wood to be mitred.

The mitre box is built up from three pieces of beech so as to form a base with two parallel sides. There are two saw cuts across the sides: each at 45 degrees to the left and right respectively.

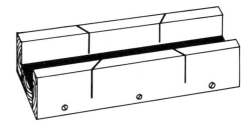

Fig. 38   Mitre box

HANDSCREW, Fig. 39

Uses. 1. For holding pieces of wood together.
    2. For fixing work to the bench.

Parts. 1. Jaws: beech
    2. Screws: beech or hornbeam

The handscrew is a useful tool for holding wood because it exerts great pressure spread over a large jaw area. The screws are usually made of hornbeam because threads formed on this wood do not easily break off or strip. The threads will work more easily if rubbed with candle grease or paraffin wax. Never use oil as this soaks into the wood and destroys it.

To set the handscrew to size, take hold of the handles and rotate them like bicycle pedals. The jaws can be quickly opened or closed by this simple action called somersaulting, Fig. 40.

To use the handscrew:

1. Open the jaws a little wider than required.
2. Place the work in the jaws.
3. Tighten up the screw in the centre.
4. Tighten up the screw at the end for an extra tight grip through leverage. Remember to undo the end screw first when removing the handscrew.

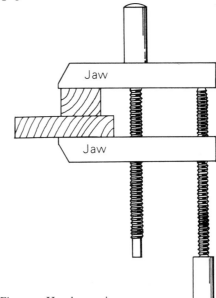

Fig. 39   Handscrew in use

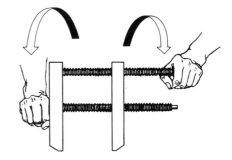

Fig. 40   The handscrew. Opening or closing by somersaulting

27

G-CRAMP, Fig. 41

This is often used in place of the hand-screw. It is smaller, and sometimes more convenient to use having only one screwed spindle.

Parts. 1. Frame: Forged steel or
                      malleable iron
     2. Spindle: Steel
     3. Handle: Steel
     4. Swivel shoe: Steel

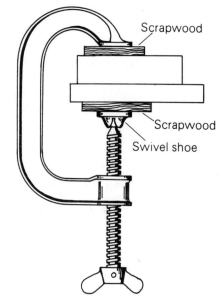

The G-cramp is especially useful for holding together small pieces of glued wood. Because this tool is made of metal, pieces of scrap wood must be used to protect the work. The cramps are made in different sizes from 50 mm to 300 mm, the size being the maximum jaw opening. In use, the handle should not be tightened too much or the frame will twist out of

Fig. 41   G-cramp

shape. As soon as the wood has been gripped, just give a slight extra turn on the handle. The swivel shoe is able to adjust itself to suit tapered pieces of wood.

SASH CRAMP, Fig. 42

Use.   For holding together glued work until the glue has set.

Parts. 1. Bar: Steel
     2. Working slide:
     3. Tail slide: Malleable iron
     4. Head:

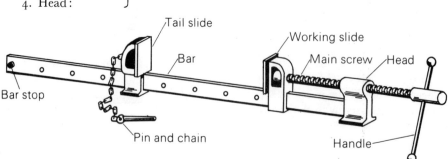

Fig. 42   Sash cramp

5. Main screw: Steel
6. Handle: Steel

The size of a sash cramp is the length of the bar and this varies from 610 mm to 1 220 mm in the lighter type of cramp, and from 610 mm to 1 524 mm in the heavier cramp.

Scrap wood

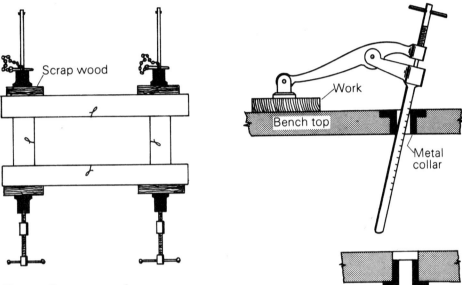

Fig. 43 Frame cramped up

Work
Bench top
Metal collar
A quick method of fixing the collar is to screw it under the bench. This method also keeps the collar away from edge tools

Fig. 44 Holdfast

Normally, at least two sash cramps should be used, one at each end of the work to hold it together, Fig. 43. On large work, it might be necessary to use four or more sash cramps. Scrap wood must always be used to protect the work from the metal slides.

On a small project using two sash cramps proceed as follows:

1. Assemble the work dry, that is, without any glue.
2. Wind the working slide right back to the head on each cramp.
3. Move the tail slides to the end of the bar.
4. Stand the cramps on their bases and place the work across the bars.
5. Place soft scrap wood between the slides and the project.
6. Move the tail slides up to the work and push the pins in the nearest holes. These will hold the tail slides in position on the bars.

7. Now wind the working slides forward until they just grip the scrap wood and the work. Tighten each cramp a little at a time to keep the work square.
8. Tighten each cramp gently. Do not over tighten — you may bend or twist the work out of shape.

Now that everything has been checked, undo the cramps, glue the work and replace it on the sash cramp bars. Quickly tighten up the cramps and test that the work is held true and square. Wipe off surplus glue and leave until the glue has set.

Notice that we should always have a trial run before gluing up. This enables us to find out any difficulties which there may be and gives us a chance to correct them. On some awkward jobs a trial run is essential so that we can learn the best method of gluing and cramping up the work.

HOLDFAST, Fig. 44
This is a useful tool for holding wood on the bench.

Exercises

1. State what you believe are the three most important safety rules for your craft room.

2. Make a neat sketch of a bench stop you have used. If you think it could be improved make a second sketch to show this.

3. Why is your bench vice faced with wood? Name the wood used for facing and give reasons for its choice.

4. What is meant by 'shooting' or 'shuting'?

5. Describe how you would make a bench hook (or sawing board). Use the following headings:

   (a) Materials required
   (b) Method of assembly
   (c) Details of joints
   (d) Dimensional sketch of complete job
   (e) Important features to consider so that the job will be serviceable.

   (ASSOCIATED LANCASHIRE SCHOOLS EXAMINING BOARD)

6. Name three kinds of cramps you use in your woodwork shop.
   (SOUTH-EAST REGIONAL EXAMINATIONS BOARD)

5
Marking Out and Testing Tools

WINDING STICKS, Fig. 45

Use. For testing a piece of wood to see whether it is flat or in winding, which means twisted. Winding sticks consist of two straight lengths of wood with their long edges parallel. On each stick one of these long edges is bevelled.

To use winding sticks:
1. Place the wood to be tested flat on a bench.
2. Place the winding sticks across the wood, one near each end.
3. Stand a few feet away.
4. Bend down until you see the two bevelled edges almost in line with each other.

If the two edges are parallel then the wood is flat. If the two edges are not parallel the wood is in winding and the high parts must be planed off. The edges of winding sticks can be seen more clearly if each stick is of a different colour.

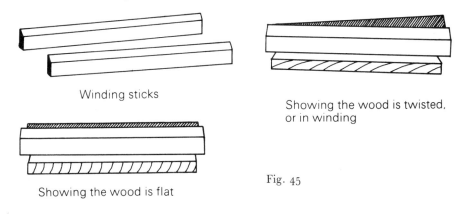

Winding sticks

Showing the wood is twisted, or in winding

Showing the wood is flat

Fig. 45

RULE, Fig. 46

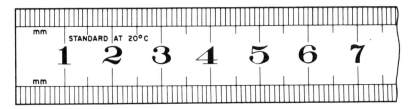

mm
STANDARD AT 20°C
1 2 3 4 5 6 7
mm

Fig. 46

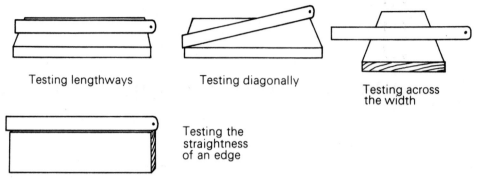

Testing lengthways   Testing diagonally

Testing across
the width

Testing the
straightness
of an edge

Uses. 1. For measuring
        2. For testing a flat surface
        3. For testing a straight edge

A rule is made of tool steel, hardened, and spring tempered.

TRY SQUARE, Fig. 47

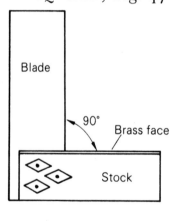

Blade

90°

Brass face

Stock

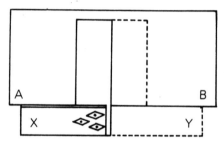

A

B

X   Y

Testing accuracy of square: place square
in position X against straight edge of
wood A–B Mark line on wood Now place
square in position Y when blade should
line up with marked line

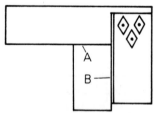

A
B

Edge A is being tested for
squareness to edge B

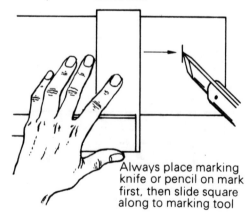

Always place marking
knife or pencil on mark
first, then slide square
along to marking tool

Fig. 47 Try square

Uses. 1. For testing that one surface is square to another. Square means at right-angles or 90 degrees.

2. For marking out lines which must be square to the edge of the wood.

Parts. 1. Blade — steel, blued to prevent rusting.

2. Stock — rosewood, brass-faced to reduce wear.

3. Rivets — for holding the stock and blade together.

Using the try square:

1. Hold the work in the left hand up to the light.

2. Place the stock against the face side and slide it down until the blade touches the edge.

3. If no light shows under the blade, the work is square. The work should be tested in several places along its length.

The try square must be handled with care for it will only work accurately if the blade is square to the stock. Banging and dropping it will loosen the rivets.

SLIDING BEVEL, Fig. 48

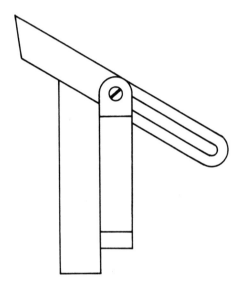

Uses. 1. For testing two flat surfaces meeting at an angle other than 90 degrees.

2. For marking out lines which are not at right-angles to the edge of the wood.

Parts. 1. Blade—steel, slotted to allow it to slide.

2. Stock—rosewood, with brass ends for protection.

3. Either a screw or lever lock nut —for locking the blade in position.

A bevel is a sloping edge and its accuracy can only be tested with a sliding bevel. The size of the tool is known by the blade length, 190 mm being suitable for school use.

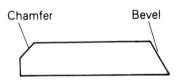

Chamfer   Bevel

Fig. 48   Sliding bevel in use

MITRE SQUARE, Fig. 49

Uses. 1. For marking out angles of 45 and 135 degrees.

2. For testing mitres.

33

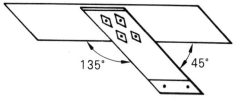

Fig. 49   Mitre square

Parts. 1. Blade — steel, fixed at an angle of 45 degrees.
      2. Stock — rosewood.
      3. Rivets — for securing the blade to the stock.
A mitre is a bevel which slopes at 45 degrees.

Fig. 50   Marking knife in use

MARKING KNIFE, Fig. 50

Use.   For marking lines on wood, usually across the grain.
Parts. 1. Blade — steel, hardened and tempered and sharpened to a cutting edge.
      2. Handle — hardwood, riveted to the blade.

A pencil makes a thick line so is no use for accurate marking out. A marking knife cuts a thin line in the wood and is very much better. It is nearly always used with the try square. The marking knife is first placed on the mark, then the try square is moved along to touch it. By this method the line is cut in the exact place.

MARKING GAUGE, Fig. 51

Uses. 1. For marking parallel lines along the grain.
      2. For marking wood to width and thickness.
Parts. 1. Stem—beech
      2. Stock—beech
      3. Thumbscrew—boxwood or plastic
      4. Spur—hardened steel

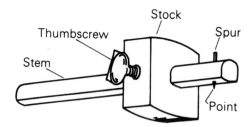

Fig. 51   Marking gauge

The marking gauge is set to size by using a rule and sliding the stock along the stem, Fig. 52. When the stock face is the required distance from the spur point the thumbscrew is lightly tightened. The size is checked and any necessary adjustment made by tapping the stem end on the bench. Finally, the thumbscrew is tightened.

In use, the marking gauge is held in the right hand, and must be pressed firmly

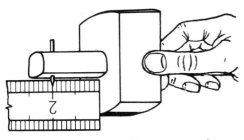

Fig. 52   Setting the marking gauge to size

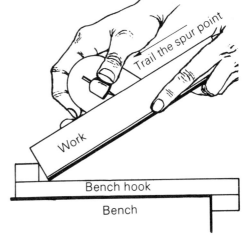

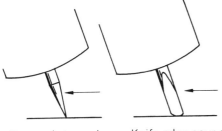

Fig. 53   Marking gauge in use

Spur point wanders with the grain

Knife edge spur cuts through the grain and results in a straight line

Fig. 54

against the edge of the wood with the gauge tilted forward to let the spur point trail, Fig. 53. It will then leave a mark along the wood as the gauge is moved forward. Beginners find this tool difficult to use, but it helps if the wood is secured in the vice or held with one end of the bench hook.

On some softwoods the spur point tends to drift with the grain instead of marking a straight line. This can be overcome by sharpening the point on both sides to produce a knife edge. If the knife edge is set at a slight angle to the face of the stock, the gauging action will tend to draw the stock against the edge of the wood, Fig. 54.

CUTTING GAUGE, **Fig. 55**

Uses. 1. For marking parallel lines across the grain.
   2. For cutting small rebates.
   3. For cutting thin strips of wood such as balsa.
Parts. 1. Stem — beech
   2. Stock — beech
   3. Cutter — steel, hardened and tempered.
   4. Wedge — brass, holds the cutter in place.
   5. Thumbscrew — boxwood or plastic.
The stock may be faced with brass strips to reduce wear.

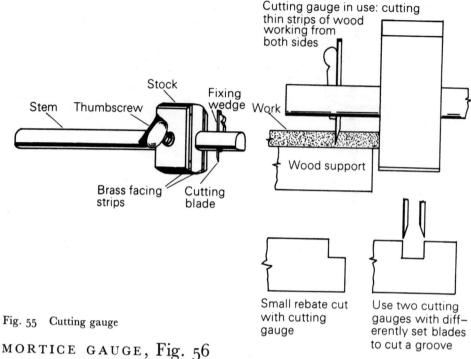

Fig. 55 Cutting gauge

MORTICE GAUGE, Fig. 56

Use. For marking double lines parallel to
an edge as for the width of mortices.

Parts. 1. Stock — rosewood, with brass
facing strips.
  2. Stem — rosewood
  3. Fixed spur — hardened steel
  4. Adjustable spur — hardened steel
  5. Adjusting screw — for setting the
spurs to size.
  6. Set screw — for locking the stock
to the stem.

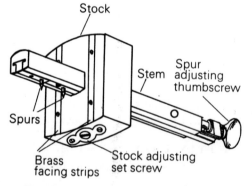

Fig. 56

The main purpose of the mortice gauge
is to mark the thickness of a mortice and
tenon joint. Chisels vary slightly in size and for this reason the chisel should be selected
first. Then proceed as follows:
1. Set the spur points to the width of the chisel, Fig. 57.
2. Set the stock to the required distance from the spurs and lightly tighten in place.
3. Check the setting and adjust if necessary, Fig. 58.
4. Tighten the set screw.

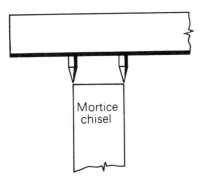

Fig. 57 Setting spurs to mortice chisel. The points should meet the ends of the chisel

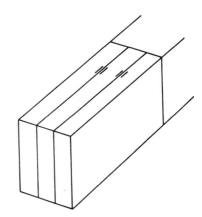

Fig. 58 Setting the spurs to the middle of the wood: set them as near as possible, make a short mark from both sides, then set between these marks

THUMB GAUGE, Fig. 59

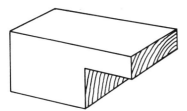

Fig. 59 Thumb gauge

Mark out chamfers with a pencil. A marking gauge leaves cut lines on the finished work

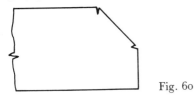

Fig. 60

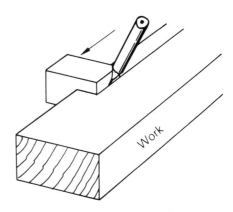

Fig. 61 Thumb gauge in use

Use. For drawing pencil lines parallel to an edge.

If we marked out a chamfer with a cut line it would still show after the chamfer had been made and would spoil the appearance of the work, Fig. 60. For this reason we use a pencil to mark out a chamfer and this is used with a thumb gauge to keep the line straight, Fig. 61.

The thumb gauge is a simple tool and can be made from scrap wood.

37

WING COMPASSES, Fig. 62

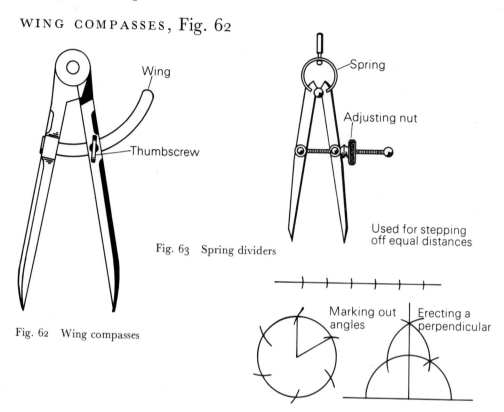

Wing

Thumbscrew

Fig. 62   Wing compasses

Fig. 63   Spring dividers

Spring

Adjusting nut

Used for stepping
off equal distances

Marking out
angles

Erecting a
perpendicular

Uses.   1. For marking out circles and arcs.

2. For stepping off distances along a line.

Parts.   1. Legs—bridle-jointed at one end, pointed at the other.

2. Wing — steel.

3. Thumbscrew—steel, locks the legs in position.

Spring dividers are used for marking out smaller circles, Fig. 63. Useful sizes are 250 mm for wing compasses and 150 mm for spring dividers, the size being the distance from the joint to the leg points.

TRAMMELS, Fig. 64

Use. For marking out large arcs and circles beyond the scope of the dividers. Beams are available for work up to 1 800 mm radius.

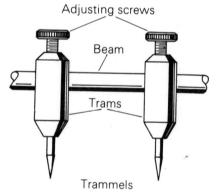

Adjusting screws

Beam

Trams

Trammels

Fig. 64   Trammels

Exercises

1. How would you test the surface of a piece of wood to see whether it was twisted or flat?

2. Name three testing tools. State how and when each would be used.

3. Make neat sketches to show the difference between a bevel and a chamfer.

4. Name three marking out tools. State how and when each would be used.

5. How are the spurs of a mortice gauge set to size?

6. Make a neat sketch of a thumb gauge and state when you would use it.

7. Make a sketch of a woodworker's try square and name the various parts. Mention the material and the purpose of each part. Explain briefly, with the help of sketches, how to check the accuracy of the square. What would be the likely causes of any inaccuracy?
(ASSOCIATED LANCASHIRE SCHOOLS EXAMINING BOARD)

8. Name the gauge that you would use to mark:
   (a) a line parallel to the edge of a board;
   (b) two lines parallel to each other and parallel to the edge.
(SOUTHERN REGIONAL EXAMINATIONS BOARD)

6

Handsaws and their Use

Handsaws

Use. For the sawing of large pieces of timber.
There are three kinds of handsaw:
1. Rip saw.
2. Cross cut saw.
3. Panel saw.

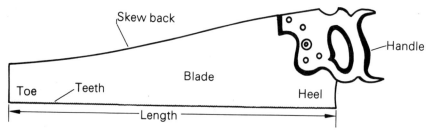

Fig. 65   Handsaw

Parts. Fig. 65
1. *Blade:* This is made of good quality tool steel, hardened and spring tempered all over.
2. *Teeth:* These are cut along the front edge of the blade. They vary in size and shape according to the type of saw.
3. *Handle:* This is usually made of beech because it is a hard, strong, close grained wood. The handle is fixed to the blade with brass screws and nuts.

SIZE

The size of a handsaw is the length of its cutting edge and also the number of teeth points per 25 mm. This number is always one more than the number of teeth per 25 mm because the first and last points are counted, Fig. 66. On most handsaws this number is stamped on the heel of the blade.

Handsaws vary in length from 458 mm

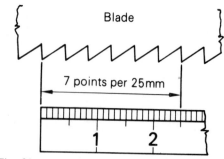

Fig. 66

40

to 712 mm. The following table shows the different sizes of the various handsaws:

SAW	LENGTH	POINTS PER 25 mm
Rip	660 mm or 712 mm	5
Cross-cut	610 mm or 660 mm	6, 7, or 8
Panel	458 mm, 508 mm, or 559 mm	10 or 12

SET, Fig. 67

Each tooth is bent for half its depth alternately to the right and left. This is called the set. It prevents the saw blade from jamming in the cut or kerf and also enables each tooth to cut. Setting must be kept as small as possible to keep the saw cut narrow. This reduces the timber wastage as well as the sawing effort. Most saw blades are also tapered in thickness from the toothed edge to the back for increased blade clearance in the kerf.

Handsaw blades may be obtained straight-backed or skew-backed and although this shape has nothing to do with the efficiency of the saw, the skew back is the more popular in Britain. Soon, however, it is expected that mass production methods will supply only the straight-back blade.

PITCH, Fig. 68

To make the saw cut smoothly the front faces or edges of the teeth slope forward. This slope is called the pitch and varies from about 3 degrees for rip saws to 14 degrees for cross-cut saws.

RIP SAW, Fig. 69

Use. For ripping or sawing along the grain.

The teeth are flat-faced and cut like chisels, the waste wood falling out as shavings. This saw will not cut properly across the grain because the teeth will tear the fibres.

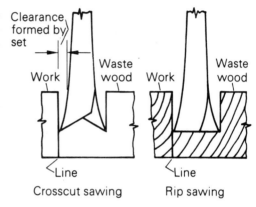

Fig. 67

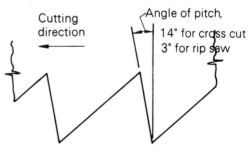

Fig. 68   Pitch

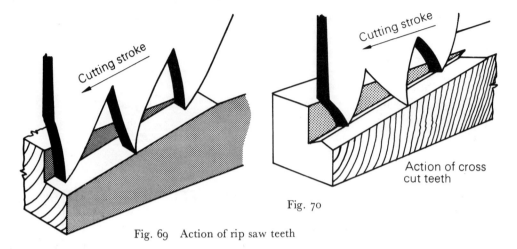

Fig. 70

Fig. 69   Action of rip saw teeth

CROSS-CUT SAW, Fig. 70

Use. For sawing across the grain.

The teeth are knife-edged with needle points so that the wood fibres are cleanly cut. The wood in the middle of the kerf then crumbles out as sawdust. This saw can be used for cutting along the grain, but is slower and less efficient than the rip saw.

PANEL SAW

Use. For sawing plywood, thin boards, and large joints.

This saw is a fine-toothed form of cross-cut saw.

SAWING FROM A BOARD

Mark out with pencil. Support the timber on trestles and kneel on it to hold it firmly. Using the left thumb as a guide draw the saw backwards several times at a low angle on the waste side of the line, Fig. 71. When a deep kerf has been made, move the left hand 50 mm or so to one side for safety. Saw lightly to deepen the kerf, then gradually raise the sawing angle to 60 degrees, Fig. 72. Use long slow strokes with slight pressure on the forward stroke only, and continue sawing along the waste side of the line. When nearing the end of the cut, saw lightly.

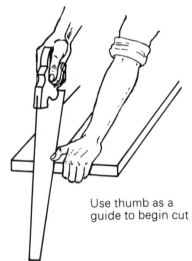

Use thumb as a guide to begin cut

Fig. 71

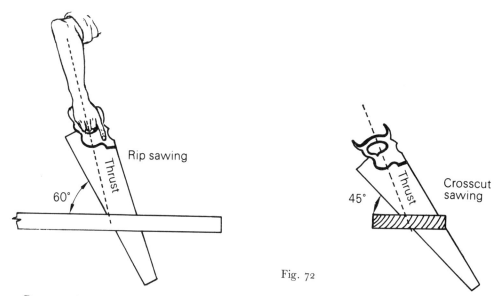

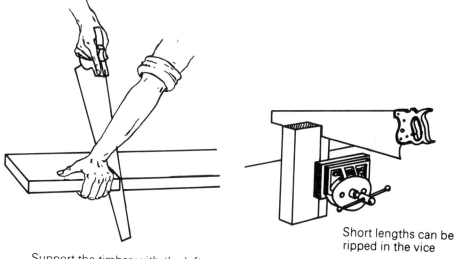

Fig. 72

Because the kerf has width, sawing must be done on the waste side of the line otherwise the timber will be under size.

Quite often, a piece of timber has to be cut out of a board. In this case, saw down the length first, gradually raising the sawing angle to 90 degrees near the end of the cut. This avoids leaving saw cuts on the board and spoiling it. The wood is then sawn across

Support the timber with the left hand when near the end of the cut to avoid splintering

Short lengths can be ripped in the vice

Fig. 73

the grain, finishing cleanly with a vertical cut. With the left hand, support the timber to prevent it from snapping off and splitting the last inch or two, Fig. 73.

TENON SAW, Fig. 74

Fig. 74   Tenon saw

Uses.   1. For sawing tenons.
       2. For sawing small pieces of wood.

Parts.   1. *Blade:* A thin short length of good quality tool steel, hardened and spring tempered all over.
       2. *Teeth:* Similar in shape to those of the cross-cut saw, but very much smaller and pitched at 16 degrees.
       3. *Back:* This is made of steel or brass. It is folded to fit tightly along the back of the blade to hold it rigid. Steel backed saws are cheap and strong but the back tends to rust. Brass backed blades are more expensive, not so strong but heavier than steel, and will not rust.
       4. *Handle:* Made of beech and secured to the blade with brass screws and nuts.

The tenon saw is made in the following sizes, but the 250 mm is large enough for the craft room.

LENGTH	POINTS PER 25 mm
254 mm	16
305 mm	14
356 mm	13

DOVETAIL SAW, Fig. 75

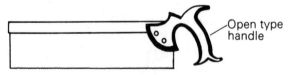

Fig. 75   Dovetail saw

Uses.   1. For sawing dovetails.
       2. For small, accurate bench work.

This saw is 204 mm long and has 20 points per 25 mm. The teeth are pitched at 16 degrees and are flat-faced to cut like rip saw teeth. This is because its main purpose is to saw along the grain for dovetailing.

The handle is similar in shape to that of the tenon saw but may be 'open' or 'closed'. Both the tenon and dovetail saws are also known as backsaws.

Saw Maintenance

After a saw has been in use for some time, the teeth become blunt. It must then be handed over to a saw doctor who will recondition it. A saw in bad condition will require the following treatment in the order given to make it as good as new:
1. Topping
2. Shaping
3. Setting
4. Sharpening

TOPPING, Fig. 76

This operation is only carried out when the teeth are uneven or broken. A flat file is used to file the tops of the teeth to form them into a straight line.

SHAPING, Fig. 77

The teeth are filed to a uniform shape, size and pitch by using a smooth three-square file. The tip of each tooth will then end in a sharp edge or point.

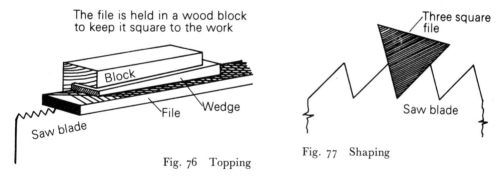

Fig. 76   Topping

Fig. 77   Shaping

SETTING, Fig. 78

The saw is placed on a block of steel or hardwood having a chamfered edge. Half the depth of each alternate tooth is slightly bent down on the chamfer by tapping it with a cross pein hammer. After completing one side, the blade is turned over and the other teeth are bent down or set. There are also a number of specially designed saw-setting tools on the market which can be used instead of the hammer and block.

SHARPENING, Fig. 79

There are two distinct methods of sharpening, one for the cross-cut and the other for the rip saw. In both cases the tops of the teeth are lightly filed to produce small, shiny flat

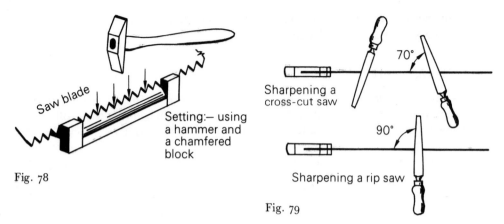

Setting:— using a hammer and a chamfered block

Fig. 78

Sharpening a cross-cut saw

Sharpening a rip saw

Fig. 79

surfaces called 'shiners'. These act as a guide by showing how much filing has to be done.

For cross-cut saws, each alternate gullet is filed two or three times at an angle of 70 degrees to the blade length. This forms a bevelled edge on the teeth. A small, three-square file is used and filing should reduce the 'shiner' to half its size. After completing one side, the saw blade is reversed and the remaining gullets filed to remove all 'shiners'.

The rip saw is filed at right-angles to the blade length to produce chisel-like teeth.

BOW SAW, Fig. 80

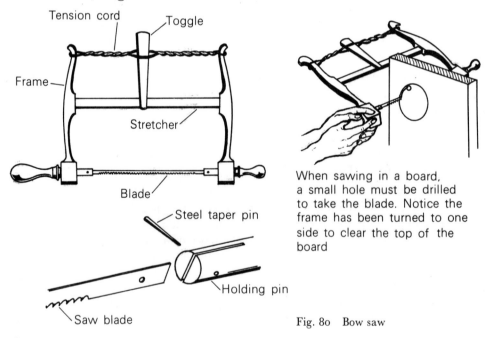

Tension cord

Toggle

Frame

Stretcher

Blade

Steel taper pin

Holding pin

Saw blade

When sawing in a board, a small hole must be drilled to take the blade. Notice the frame has been turned to one side to clear the top of the board

Fig. 80   Bow saw

46

Use. For the sawing of curves in wood about 13 mm thick and above.

Parts. 1. Two arms ⎤
     2. Stretcher ⎥
              ⎬ beech
     3. Toggle ⎥
     4. Two handles ⎦
     5. Holding pins — brass
     6. Cord

To keep the blade rigid in use it is tensioned by winding the toggle round several times causing the cord to stretch the frame. A slack blade cannot saw and will soon break.

Both handles are free to rotate in the arms but should be turned together to keep the blade straight. This allows the frame to be moved to any convenient position when following a curve. For internal curves, a hole must be bored first in the waste wood. This is for the blade to pass through after which it is assembled in the frame and tensioned. When sawing, the right-hand should grip the longer handle with the left-hand overlapping the right. The blades are made in four sizes and have teeth of rip saw pattern.

PAD SAW, Fig. 81

Use. For sawing slots and curves too far from the edge of wood for the bow saw to reach.

Parts. 1. Handle — beech.
     2. Blade holder — a hollow casting with two screws for holding the blade.
     3. Blade — tool steel with teeth of rip saw pattern.

The blade is tapered in width and made in six sizes, from 204 mm to 356 mm long. To prevent breakage, the blades are tempered softer than usual so that they will bend instead of breaking if forced too hard, and can be straightened again quite easily. The handle is hollow to take the blade which should be fixed with the least possible length projecting. This helps to prevent the blade from buckling in use.

Set screws holding the blade

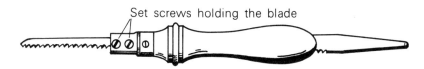

Fig. 81   Pad saw

COPING SAW, Fig. 82

Use. For sawing curved shapes in thin wood.

Parts. 1. Steel frame
     2. Plain rear pin
     3. Screwed front pin

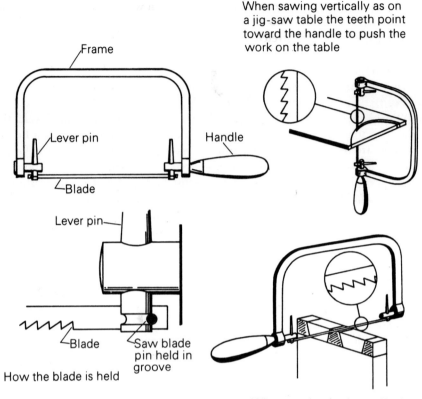

Frame

Lever pin

Handle

Blade

When sawing vertically as on a jig-saw table the teeth point toward the handle to push the work on the table

Lever pin

Blade

Saw blade pin held in groove

How the blade is held

When sawing horizontally, the teeth should point away from the handle

Fig. 82   Coping saw

    4. Screwed handle
    5. Lever pins.

The coping saw is a miniature form of bow saw. The blade is 165 mm long and has teeth of rip saw pattern. The blade can be turned to any position by means of the levers.

In use, the work is held on a wooden table and the saw used vertically with the teeth pointing downwards. For normal use at the vice the teeth should point away from the handle to cut on the push stroke. Because the frames are not perfectly rigid in use there is a danger of blade breakage so the blade is sometimes reversed to cut on the pull stroke. This method causes the wood to splinter on the face making it difficult to follow the line.

Because the bow, pad, and coping saws are used to cut wood across the grain as well as with it, their teeth should be of cross-cut form for clean cutting. It is not clear why they are not, but it may be the manufacturing methods of a low-priced item, and tradition, but it is worth noting that it is common practice in industry to lightly file the teeth to cross-cut form.

Exercises

1. A handsaw may be said to have 8 points per 25 mm. What does this mean?

2. What is meant by 'set'? What is the purpose of 'set'?

3. Describe briefly, the four main steps in re-sharpening a badly worn saw.

4. When would you use: (a) a bow saw, (b) a coping saw?

5. Explain, with the aid of sketches, how the cutting action of a cross-cut saw differs from that of rip saw.

(EAST ANGLIAN REGIONAL EXAMINATIONS BOARD)

6. By means of a sketch and notes show clearly why it is advisable when sawing to a line to saw on the waste wood side of the line.

(WEST MIDLANDS EXAMINATIONS BOARD)

7. Name two points to bear in mind when using a coping saw so as to prevent the blade from breaking. Give two examples where you would use this saw.

(WELSH JOINT EDUCATION COMMITTEE)

8. Which saw is normally used for bench work?

(EAST ANGLIAN REGIONAL EXAMINATIONS BOARD)

7

Planes

The direction in which the fibres lie is called the grain, Fig. 83. In some trees the grain is straight so that the wood is easy to work, but very often the fibres grow at an angle or follow a wavy path. Although this irregular way of growing produces attractive looking wood it is often difficult to plane and chisel to a smooth finish.

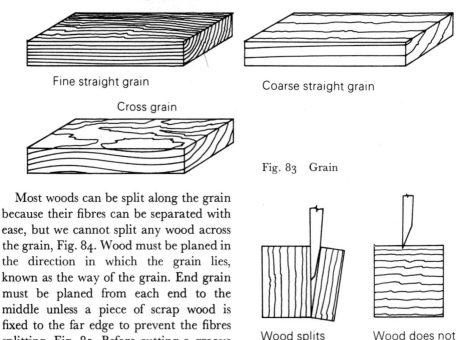

Fine straight grain

Cross grain

Coarse straight grain

Fig. 83 Grain

Most woods can be split along the grain because their fibres can be separated with ease, but we cannot split any wood across the grain, Fig. 84. Wood must be planed in the direction in which the grain lies, known as the way of the grain. End grain must be planed from each end to the middle unless a piece of scrap wood is fixed to the far edge to prevent the fibres splitting, Fig. 85. Before cutting a groove across the grain a saw cut must be made down either side of the groove to sever the fibres which can then be removed with a chisel, Fig. 86.

Wood splits easily along the grain

Wood does not split across the grain

Fig. 84

When you understand this you have learned the three important rules in cutting wood:
1. Always plane the way of the grain.
2. Always make saw cuts before chiselling across the grain.
3. Never plane right across end grain.

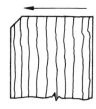

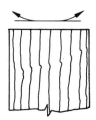

| Planing end grain right across splits the end of the wood— | This can be overcome by cutting off the corner— | A better method is to glue or cramp a piece of scrapwood to the end and cut off its corner— | Or avoid the end by planing two thirds of the way from each end |

Fig. 85

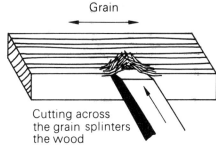
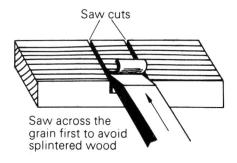

Grain

Saw cuts

Cutting across the grain splinters the wood

Saw across the grain first to avoid splintered wood

Fig. 86

Planes

JACK PLANE, Fig. 87

Use. For planing a piece of timber almost to size.

Parts. 1. Body — beech
2. Handle — beech
3. Cutting iron — hardened steel
4. Cap iron — steel
5. Wedge — beech
6. Striking button — boxwood

The wooden jack plane is 356 mm long and has a 50 mm wide blade. The blade is held in the plane body at an angle known as the pitch. In the jack plane, the pitch is 45 degrees so that in action the blade half cuts and half scrapes. A higher angle than this would cause the blade to scrape entirely.

The cutting iron is ground and sharpened so that the blade edge is slightly curved, Fig. 88. This enables thick shavings to be cut more easily and avoids marking the surface of the wood with the corners of the iron.

When we begin to plane, the cutting iron lifts a shaving of wood. This tries to split

51

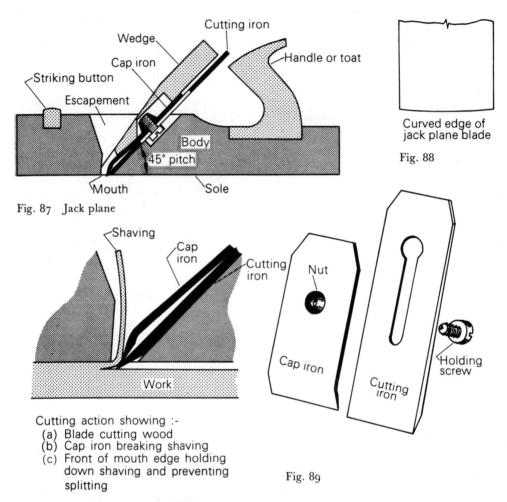

Fig. 88 Curved edge of jack plane blade

Fig. 87 Jack plane

Cutting action showing :-
 (a) Blade cutting wood
 (b) Cap iron breaking shaving
 (c) Front of mouth edge holding down shaving and preventing splitting

Fig. 89

along the grain but is stopped by the front of the plane mouth. Even so, there is some splitting. To stop this a cap or back iron is fitted to the cutting iron, Fig. 89. The cap iron breaks the shaving so that it has no power to tear and split the wood. The cap iron also strengthens the cutting iron and holds it rigid while planing.

Planing

The plane is held in two hands and pushed along the wood in the direction of the grain. Normally, planing should start near one long edge so that the shavings are removed in parallel rows as the plane is worked across to the other edge. If the wood is twisted, then planing must first go from high corner to high corner. Keep testing with a rule to see that the work is straight and flat.

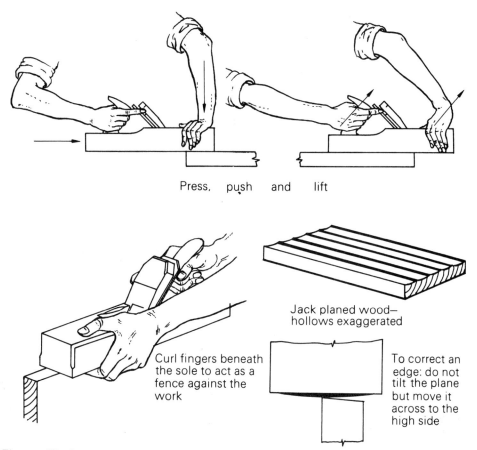

Press, push and lift

Jack planed wood—
hollows exaggerated

Curl fingers beneath
the sole to act as a
fence against the
work

To correct an
edge: do not
tilt the plane
but move it
across to the
high side

Fig. 90 Planing

Once, all planes were made of beech because it is a hard, close-grained timber. It slides easily over wood and is light in weight, but the method of setting the irons is difficult and the size of the mouth cannot be adjusted.

Today, the metal plane is very popular, Fig. 91. The mouth can be set to different sizes and the depth of cut can be easily altered by means of a knurled wheel. Unfortunately, the metal plane is heavier than the wooden one and it may break if dropped on the floor. It does not slide very well on wood, especially resinous timbers, but this can be remedied by rubbing the metal sole with paraffin wax. Metal planes are also made with corrugated bases to make them slide more easily.

When planing timber with a twisted grain it is important to narrow the mouth of the plane and set the cap iron close to the cutting edge of the blade. This prevents the

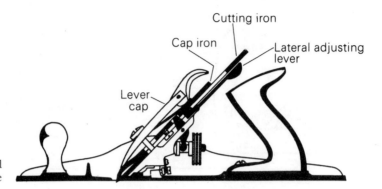

Fig. 91
The metal
jack plane

shavings from tearing out and spoiling the surface of the wood. The adjustable mouth is a great advantage of the metal plane.

TRY PLANE, Fig. 92

Use. For truing up large surfaces and long edges.

The name of this tool is really a 'truing' plane, but like many other words it has become changed over the years. It is similar to the jack plane except for two things:

1. The sole is longer for accurate long work.
2. The cutting edge is ground and sharpened quite straight, but the corners are rounded off so as not to leave marks on the work surface.

After using the jack plane for the bulk of the planing, the try plane is used to make the surface flat and true. For planing long edges this plane is excellent. If the plane is set 'fine', that is, set to remove a very thin shaving, then the long sole will make the plane cut a flat surface or a straight edge, Fig. 93.

For greater accuracy when joining the edges of boards, a still longer plane is used. This is called a jointer, and wooden jointers vary from 660 mm to 762 mm in length. Metal planes are not made as long

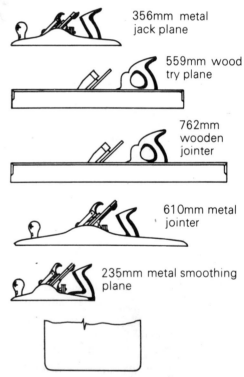

356mm metal jack plane

559mm wood try plane

762mm wooden jointer

610mm metal jointer

235mm metal smoothing plane

Try, jointer and smoothing plane blades have a straight cutting edge. The corners are usually rounded to avoid marking the work

Fig. 92   Relative sizes of planes

as this and manufacturers no longer refer to the try plane. Instead, they list the metal jointer which is made in two sizes, 559 mm and 610 mm, Fig. 92.

SMOOTHING PLANE, Fig. 94

Use. For smoothing wood after the jack or try plane has been used.

You may remember that the jack plane is used for planing wood almost to size. This is because we must allow for a thin shaving to be removed from all over the wood when the work is complete. The purpose of this is to leave the finished job clean and smooth from all the previous tool marks and for this we use a smoothing plane.

The smoothing plane is smaller than the jack plane, but the cutting edge is ground and sharpened straight like the try plane. Because of its small size this plane is very popular and one often sees it used for general planing of all kinds. This is wrong because the finely set blade should only be used for cleaning up work and also the short length of sole will not produce a flat surface.

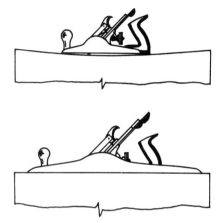

A short soled plane with a coarse set blade will plane hollow

A long soled plane with a fine set blade will plane straight and flat

Fig. 93

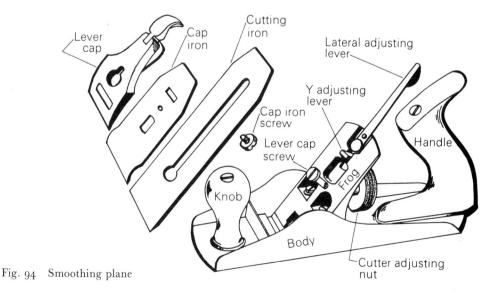

Fig. 94   Smoothing plane

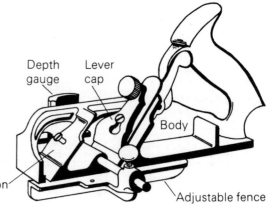

Depth gauge   Lever cap

Body

Fig. 95 Rebate   Bullnose position   Adjustable fence
and fillister plane   (seldom used)

REBATE AND FILLISTER PLANE, Fig. 95

Uses. 1. When fitted with the depth gauge and fence the tool becomes a fillister plane and is used for making rebates.

2. Without the depth gauge and fence the tool is a rebate plane and is used for trimming and finishing off rebates.

Parts. 1. Body — cast iron
2. Fence — cast iron
3. Cutter — alloy tool steel
4. Lever cap — cast iron
5. Depth gauge — cast iron
6. Spur — hardened steel.

A step cut along the edge of a piece of wood is called a rebate, rabbit, or rabbet, Fig. 96.

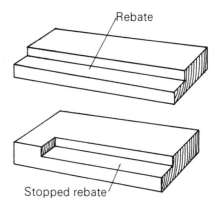

Rebate

Stopped rebate

Fig. 96

The plane mouth runs the full width of the sole and the cutter should project on each side of the body by an amount equal to the thickness of a piece of paper. The fence is set to the width and a depth gauge fixes the depth of the rebate, Fig. 97. Start rebating with short strokes at the end of the wood and gradually work back until shavings are being removed from the full length of the rebate, Fig. 98. Hold the plane upright and keep the fence close against the wood throughout each stroke. When rebating across the grain the small spur should be used, Fig. 99. Begin by drawing the plane back across the wood a few times to let the spur cut the fibres, then work the rebate as before. Just before completing the rebate remove the spur to avoid a cut line showing on the wood.

For accuracy, the rebate should be marked out with the marking gauge along the

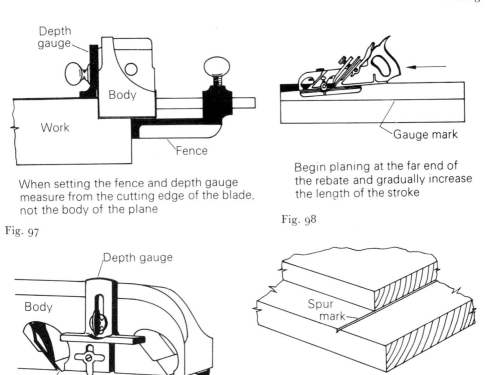

When setting the fence and depth gauge measure from the cutting edge of the blade, not the body of the plane

Fig. 97

Begin planing at the far end of the rebate and gradually increase the length of the stroke

Fig. 98

Cutting spur fitted with three blades and one neutral position

When rebating all round wood, remove spur before the last few cuts to avoid marking the work as shown

Fig. 99

grain or the cutting gauge if across the grain. The fence and depth gauge should then be set to 'scant' sizes and the rebate finished off with the rebate plane.

The forward cutting position, known as the bull-nose position, enables the plane to cut close up to the end of a stopped rebate, that is, a rebate which does not run the length of the wood. A stopped rebate must first have the stopped end cut to size with a chisel. This makes room for the plane body at the end of each stroke.

Once, glass windows were held in place by fillets of wood called filletsters. Later, these became known as fillisters and was the name given to the rebates for holding the glass. The plane used for cutting these rebates on sash windows was called a sash fillister. The special point about these rebates is that they were cut on the side opposite to the face side, so the plane depth gauge had to be on the same side as the fence.

Today, nearly all joinery is machine made and the hand methods have almost disappeared so that the true meaning of the word fillister has gone.

SHOULDER PLANE, Fig. 100

Uses. 1. For trimming the shoulders of large tenons.
2. For light work in rebates.
3. For planing end grain and fine work in general.

Parts. 1. Body — cast iron
2. Cutting iron — alloy tool steel
3. Lever cap — cast iron

Because the shoulder plane is often used on rebates it is also known as a shoulder rabbet plane.

The base of the body is ground true and square to the parallel sides resulting in accurate work in corners, and the blade is pitched at 20 degrees with the bevel upwards.

When not in use, the lever cap should be slackened off to prevent distorting the body.

BULL-NOSE PLANE, Fig. 101

Uses. 1. For work smaller than that for which the shoulder plane would be used.
2. For working in corners, stopped chamfers, and stopped rebates.

Parts. 1. Body — cast iron
2. Cutting iron — alloy tool steel
3. Lever cap — cast iron

There are two types of bull-nose plane, one having the body cast in one piece so that the mouth size is fixed and the other having an adjustable nose giving four different mouth settings.

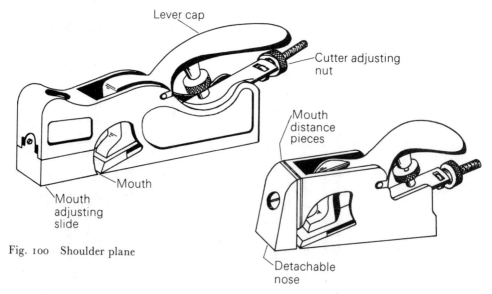

Fig. 100 Shoulder plane

Fig. 101 Bull-nose rabbet plane

Because of its small size this is a very popular plane for all kinds of small work, and is used much more than the heavier shoulder plane.

PLOUGH PLANE, **Fig.** 102

Uses. 1. For ploughing grooves in wood.
         2. For cutting rebates.
Parts. 1. Body — cast iron
         2. Fence — cast iron
         3. Lever cap — cast iron
         4. Cutters — alloy tool steel
         5. Depth gauge — cast iron

Eight different sized cutters are normally supplied with the plough plane, and these range from 3 mm to 15 mm. The grooves can be cut to a depth of 16 mm at any distance from the edge of the wood up to 127 mm. Extra cutters of 4, 6, 9, and 12 mm can be obtained for cutting grooves to take plywood panels.

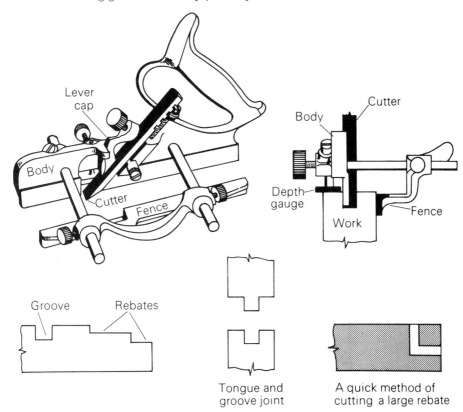

Fig. 102   The plough plane

The cutter is clamped down by the lever cap and held in place by a side screw while the depth of cut is controlled by a screw at the rear of the blade. The fence and depth gauge are set to the required sizes and ploughing begins by taking short cutting strokes at the end of the work. The strokes are gradually lengthened until shavings are being removed for the full stroke. Ploughing continues until the depth gauge is rubbing along the wood and no more shavings can be removed.

BLOCK PLANE, Fig. 103

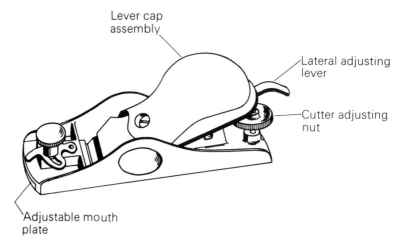

Lever cap assembly

Lateral adjusting lever

Cutter adjusting nut

Adjustable mouth plate

Fig. 103   Block plane

Use.   For small general planing work at the bench.
Parts.   1. Body — cast iron
      2. Adjustable mouth plate — cast iron
      3. Lever cap assembly — steel
      4. Cutting iron — hardened tool steel
      5. Cutter adjusting nut — steel
      6. Lateral adjusting lever — steel

After the wood has been planed to size and the constructional work begins, it is often necessary to trim different parts of the work. This is particularly so when the work is being assembled. For this, the block plane is used, and being small, it can be held in one hand and used with ease. The blade is pitched at 20 degrees and mounted with the bevel upwards. The narrow mouth and low pitched blade make the block plane a useful all round tool.

SPOKESHAVE, Fig. 104

Use.   For planing curved edges.

Parts. 1. Body   ⎱ 1 piece of cast iron or
        2. Handles ⎰ malleable cast iron
        3. Cutter — alloy tool steel
        4. Lever cap — cast iron

Spokeshaves are planes with very short bodies. There are two kinds:
1. Flat-faced, for convex shapes.
2. Round-faced, for concave shapes.

The handles may be raised or straight and the cutter, screw adjusted or not, though screw adjustment makes blade setting easier.

Normally, the body is made of cast iron, but because this is brittle, and the tool long and narrow, the better type is made of malleable cast iron. This is cast iron which has been specially heat treated to make it less brittle. One leading manufacturer enamels its spokeshaves red to denote malleable iron and blue for plain cast iron.

In use, the tool is held in the finger tips of both hands and worked away from the user with plenty of wrist movement, Fig. 105.

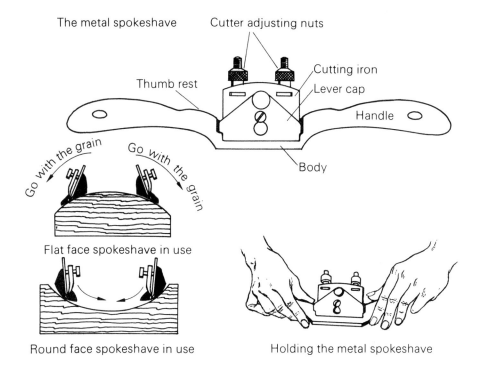

The metal spokeshave

Cutter adjusting nuts

Thumb rest

Cutting iron

Lever cap

Handle

Body

Go with the grain

Go with the grain

Flat face spokeshave in use

Round face spokeshave in use

Holding the metal spokeshave

Fig. 104   Fig. 105

ROUTER, Fig. 106

Use.   For planing the bottom of grooves, generally across the grain.

Parts. 1. Body
2. Tool clamp } cast iron
3. Tool post
4. Cutters — tool steel

After chopping out a groove with a mallet and chisel, the router is used to plane flat the bottom of the groove or trench as it is sometimes called. The tool is lightly clamped to the tool post, the blade set to the correct depth by means of the knurled wheel then locked in place by a thumbscrew.

Two cutter sizes are available, 6 mm and 13 mm, and these have straight blades for general use though a special V-shaped blade is provided for smoothing cuts.

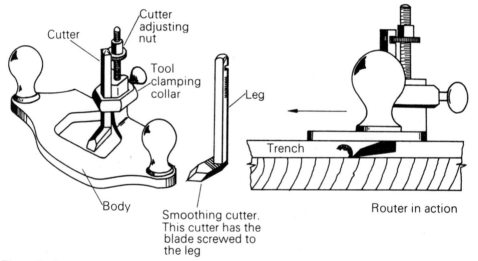

Fig. 106   Router

SCRAPER, Fig. 107

Use. To smooth the surface of hardwood by removing plane marks and torn grain.

A scraper consists of a piece of spring tempered steel usually rectangular in shape but may be curved to fit various mouldings. It is held in both hands so that the thumbs can bend it and although it is held at a scraping angle the edge is curved so that it actually cuts and produces shavings, Fig. 108. In use, the work should be scraped diagonally, first in one direction, then the other, and finally along the grain. Very often, the surface of woods having twisted, curly, or interlocked grain can only be brought to a smooth finish by means of the scraper.

To sharpen a worn scraper for use (Fig. 109):

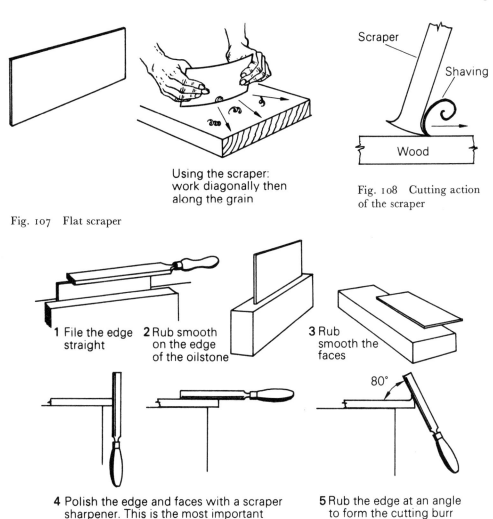

Using the scraper:
work diagonally then
along the grain

Fig. 107   Flat scraper

Scraper

Shaving

Wood

Fig. 108   Cutting action
of the scraper

1 File the edge
straight

2 Rub smooth
on the edge
of the oilstone

3 Rub
smooth the
faces

80°

4 Polish the edge and faces with a scraper
sharpener. This is the most important
stage of the sharpening

5 Rub the edge at an angle
to form the cutting burr

Fig. 109   Sharpening a worn scraper

1. Hold the scraper in a fitter's vice and file the long edge straight using a smooth file.
2. Rub the edge smooth on the side of the oilstone. Use the side because it will be flat.
3. Rub the face smooth.
4. Polish the face and edge by rubbing them with a scraper sharpener. This is called burnishing and makes the metal quite smooth. This is very important because any marks on the scraper edge will leave scratch marks all over the surface of the wood.
5. Hold the scraper on the bench or in the fitter's vice and rub the scraper sharpener

along the edge at an angle of 80 degrees to the face. Rub several times to form a burr which is the cutting edge. This burring over is performed on each side of both long edges to form four cutting edges.

If a scraper sharpener is not available the back of a 13 mm gouge will do quite well.

Scrapers are tiring to use because the blade must be sprung to shape with the thumbs. The cabinet scraper makes this unnecessary and is often preferred where much scraping has to be done. The blade is held in a cast iron body having a handle on each side and the cut is adjusted by means of a screw which bends the blade, Fig. 110.

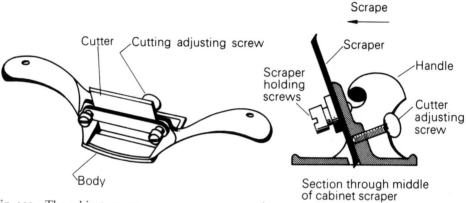

Fig. 110   The cabinet scraper

Grinding and Sharpening

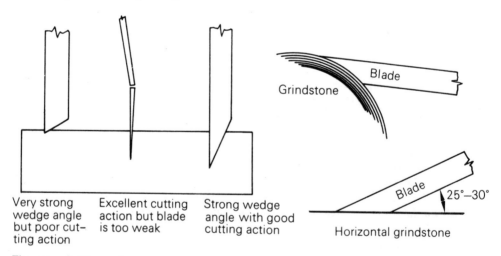

Fig. 111   Cutting action

Fig. 112   Grinding

A cutting tool is a wedge. The blade of the wedge must be kept sharp so that it will cut cleanly and with little effort. The smaller the wedge angle the more easily will it penetrate the wood, but if made too small the wedge will be weak and break in use, Fig. 111.

PLANE IRONS

To sharpen a plane iron, one side of the blade is kept flat and the other side ground on a grindstone to form a wedge angle of 25 to 30 degrees. This is called the grinding angle, Fig. 112.

The blade is then rubbed back and forth on an oilstone to form a wedge angle of 30 to 35 degrees. This is called the sharpening angle, Fig. 113. A few drops of thin machine-oil or neatsfoot oil should be used. This lubricates the stone's surface, helps the blade to move about and floats off the small particles of metal which would choke and glaze the stone.

The grinding and sharpening of the blade causes a small burr of metal to form along the cutting edge. This is known as a 'wire edge' and must be removed or it will damage the sharp edge when in use. To remove the wire edge the back of the blade must be rubbed on the fine oilstone and care must be taken to keep the blade quite flat when rubbing, Fig. 114. Some experts finish off by stropping the blade on the palm of the hand (a dangerous method for beginners), but others simply draw the edge of the blade lightly across the end grain of a piece of wood or a piece of leather to make sure that the wire edge has gone. Finally, the edge should be examined near a window. A sharp edge cannot be seen because it cannot reflect light.

From time to time the blade loses its keen edge and must be re-sharpened on the oilstone. Every time this is done the sharpened surface of the wedge gets bigger and makes sharpening a longer and slower process. When this happens the wedge is ground back to the edge and sharpening starts again. Tools are ground, therefore, simply to make sharpening easier.

If a cap iron is provided it should now be screwed to the sharpened blade. It is important to check that the edge of the cap iron fits closely along the back of the blade, Fig. 115. Any gaps will collect shavings and choke the mouth of the plane.

The edge of the cap iron should be set back from the cutting edge for different planes as follows:

Jack plane: a scant 3 mm for softwood.

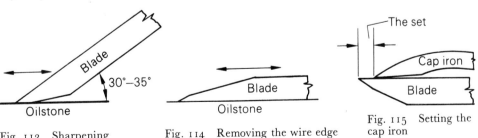

Fig. 113 Sharpening   Fig. 114 Removing the wire edge   Fig. 115 Setting the cap iron

Planes

Jack plane: 2 mm for hardwood.
Try plane and jointer: 1.5 mm
Smoothing plane: a scant 1.5 mm.
The different pitches of various planes are shown in Fig. 116.

  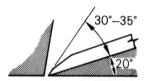

Normal pitch. This gives a half scraping, half cutting action

York pitch. This gives a scraping action and is used in smoothing planes for cleaning up twisted grain

Although the single iron pitch is only 20°, the effective pitch is 50°–55° because the blade is used bevel up

Fig. 116

Exercises

1. What is meant by grain?

2. Make a neat sketch to show the shape of the cutting edge of a jack plane. Why is this shape used?

3. Describe, with sketches, how a shaving is removed from a length of wood using a jack plane. What is the purpose of the cap or back iron?

4. What is meant by: (a) the grinding angle; (b) the sharpening angle?

5. What is the approximate angle of pitch for the cutting iron of these tools:
(a) smoothing plane; (b) shoulder plane?

(SOUTH-EAST REGIONAL EXAMINATIONS BOARD)

6. The jack plane or general purpose plane is about 400 mm long and has a blade and cap iron about 56 mm wide pitched at 45 degrees to the sole; the blade, the cutting edge of which is very slightly curved, is not the full width of the stock (or body) of the plane. Name four other types of plane used in the workshop; say how each differs from the jack plane, and give reasons for one of these differences in each case.

(WEST MIDLANDS EXAMINATIONS BOARD)

7. What is meant by each of the following terms used in your school workshop? Illustrate your answers:
(a) Cleaning up; (b) Chamfering; (c) Rebating; (d) Planing end-grain.

(EAST MIDLAND REGIONAL EXAMINATIONS BOARD)

8. Show by a diagram, why a short plane (say, a smoothing plane) used to plane the edge of a long board, could make the edge hollow.

(WEST MIDLANDS EXAMINATIONS BOARD)

9. After repeated sharpening, a scraper has become rounded on its cutting edge and needs filing flat again, so that an edge can be remade.

   Explain:
   (a) How the scraping edge can be reformed after the filing is completed.
   (b) The purpose of a scraper.

(SOUTHERN REGIONAL EXAMINATIONS BOARD)

8

Chisels and their Use: Sharpening Stones

Chisels

Uses. 1. For cutting and shaping timber where the plane cannot be used.
2. For cutting joints.

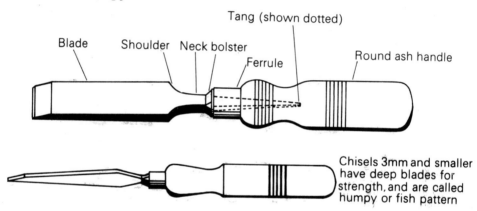

Fig. 117   The square edge firmer chisel

FIRMER CHISEL, SQUARE EDGE, Fig. 117

Parts. 1. Handle — ash, beech, or boxwood
2. Ferrule — brass or steel
3. Blade ⎱ tool steel, hardened and
4. Bolster ⎰ tempered
5. Tang — tool steel, softened

   The size of a chisel is known by the blade-width and varies from 1.5 mm to 50 mm, but from 3 mm to 25 mm is the popular range of sizes. The tang secures the blade to the handle which is fitted with a ferrule to prevent the wood splitting. In use, pressure on the handle acts on the bolster to make the blade cut. Light cutting with the chisel is called paring and the two important positions are horizontal and vertical, Fig. 118. If any great effort has to be made with the hands when using a sharp chisel, a mallet should be used for better control.

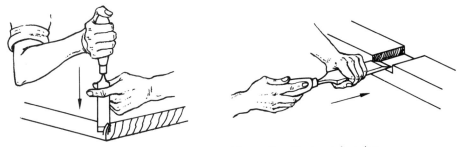

Fig. 118a   Vertical paring

Fig. 118b   Horizontal paring

The cutting edge is formed by grinding on one face only a bevel of 25 degrees then sharpening at 30 degrees. The front face of the chisel must be kept quite flat. Chisels are also obtained with a ferrule at both ends of the handle, Fig. 119. These are called registered pattern or extra strong double ferruled and are designed for use where a lot of malleting is necessary. The blades are thicker than those of the firmer chisel and a leather washer is sometimes fitted between the bolster and the handle to absorb shock.

Fig. 119   Registered chisel

FIRMER CHISEL, BEVEL EDGE, Fig. 120

This tool is similar to the square edge firmer chisel except that the back of the blade is bevelled along both edges so that it can be used in acute corners as on dovetail joints. It is a lightweight type of chisel and the mallet must be used with caution to avoid breaking the blade.

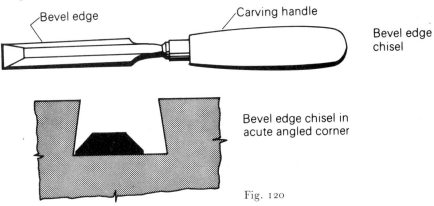

Fig. 120

69

MORTICE CHISEL, Fig. 121

This is used for cutting a mortice or slot which often forms part of a joint. The chisel for this work must be strongly made to withstand the heavy mallet blows and for use as a lever to break and remove waste. The blade thickness also prevents the chisel twisting in the mortice.

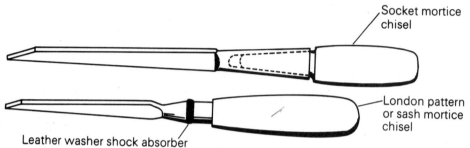

Socket mortice chisel

London pattern or sash mortice chisel

Leather washer shock absorber

Fig. 121

Gouges, Fig. 122

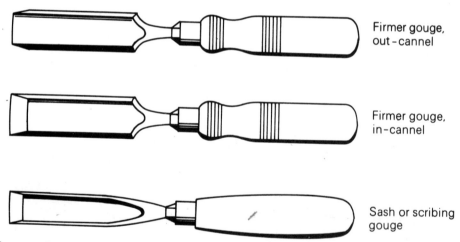

Firmer gouge, out-cannel

Firmer gouge, in-cannel

Sash or scribing gouge

Fig. 122   Gouges

A gouge is a chisel with a curved cutting edge used for hollowing. There are three kinds of gouge:

1. Firmer, out-cannel.
2. Firmer, in-cannel (often wrongly called a scribing gouge).
3. Scribing.

The cannel is the bevel, and scribing gouges are always in-cannel.

In the days of hand-made woodwork, gouges were made with six different curves ranging from 'A', almost flat, to 'F', very deep. Now that machines are widely used, the demand for all these curves has died out. Curve 'E' was the most popular and so today firmer gouges are made having only this curve or sweep. Scribing gouges are flatter and are always made to sweep 'C', Fig. 123.

Firmer gouges	Gouge size	Diam E	Gouge size	Diam C	Scribing gouges
	mm	mm	mm	mm	
	6	10	6	13	
	10	13	10	19	
	13	16	13	25	
	16	19	16	31	
	19	22	19	38	
	22	25	22	44	
	25	31	25	50	

Fig. 123   Curves of gouges

FIRMER GOUGE, OUT-CANNEL, Fig. 124

This is the most commonly used and is in demand for hollowing of all kinds from small grooves for handles to large hollows for bowls.

FIRMER GOUGE, IN-CANNEL, Fig. 125

Used for the cutting of concave outlines. This tool is difficult to grind and sharpen unless

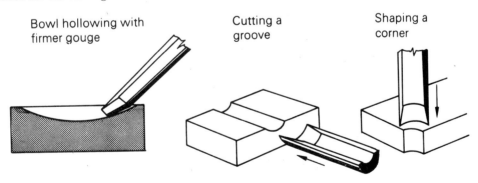

Bowl hollowing with firmer gouge

Cutting a groove

Shaping a corner

Fig. 124   Fig. 125

specially shaped oilstones are used. Even so, the sharpening of these gouges is a slow process so these tools should be treated with extra care.

SCRIBING GOUGE

This tool is used for the cutting and shaping of mouldings which have to fit together at right-angles. One part of the moulding is left whole and the other part is shaped or scribed to fit, Fig. 126. This was common practice on window frames or sashes which is why the scribing gouge is sometimes called a sash gouge.

Note particularly how gouge sizes are measured, Fig. 127.

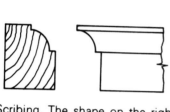

Scribing. The shape on the right has been cut, or scribed, so that it fits the part on the left. Both pieces have been cut from the same moulding

Fig. 126

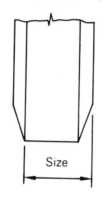

Size

Out—cannel: outside edge to inside edge

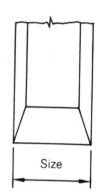

Size

In—cannel: outside edge to outside edge

Fig. 127

Mallet, Fig. 128

Uses. 1. For striking wooden handled tools.
2. For striking woodwork which must not be damaged.

Parts. 1. Head — beech
2. Handle — beech or ash

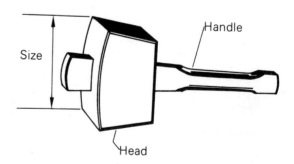

Size

Handle

Head

Fig. 128   Mallet

The handle is tapered to fit in a slot in the head so that when used, the head tightens on the handle. The angled faces ensure that the mallet squarely hits the wood. The size of a mallet is the length at the end of the head, 114 mm being light and popular.

Grindstone, Fig. 129

The grindstone used in the woodwork room usually consists of a shaped block of sandstone mounted to run in a trough.

Grinding must be done wet, that is with a good supply of water, and so a can from which water can drip when required, is placed on top of the guard. Not only does the water cool the blade and keep it hard, but it also washes away the steel grindings which would clog the stone and glaze it. After use, the water which has collected in the trough should be drained off. If the stone is left standing in water for a long time it will become soft in places and wear unevenly.

A new type of grinding machine with an artificial stone mounted horizontally is fast becoming popular, Fig. 130. The blade is mounted in the tool rest, set to the correct grinding angle and rubbed on the revolving wheel while being cooled and washed with a special honing oil. In this type of grindstone the wheel always runs true and a greater degree of control and accuracy is possible. Also the machine is compact and there is no problem of rusting.

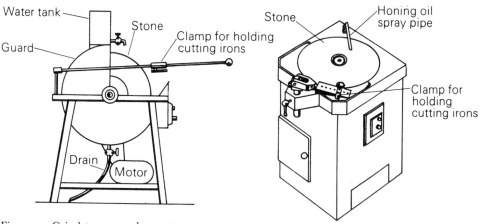

Fig. 129   Grindstone—sandstone type

Fig. 130   Horizontal grindstone

Oilstones, Fig. 131

An oilstone is used for producing a sharp edge on a tool. All grinding and sharpening scratches the metal and leaves a jagged cutting edge. The smoother the stone the finer the scratches and sharper the cutting edge. The stone may be natural like the hard

Arkansas which is quarried in America and
consists of fine particles called grit, or it
may be artificial like the Norton India
stones which are made from alundum.
This is a hard aluminium oxide made in
the electric furnace. The important advantage of the artificial stone is that its
hardness, grit size, and texture are uniform throughout. Three grit sizes are
available, coarse, medium, and fine, and
the stones are made in different sizes and
shapes. For normal use, two stones, one
fine and one medium, each measuring

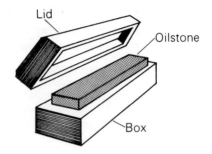

Fig. 131

200 mm by 50 mm by 25 mm, are required. Each stone should be bedded in a little
plaster of paris in a wooden box and secured to a zinc topped bench reserved for tool
sharpening. Lids should be provided and after use, the stones must be wiped clean,
lightly oiled to prevent them going hard and dry and covered to protect from dust.
Although India oilstones are saturated with oil during manufacture a little oil must
always be used when sharpening. The best is an animal oil called neatsfoot, but thin
machine oil to which a little paraffin has been added is quite suitable. Heavy oil and
grease should never be used because they
would choke the pores.

Tools should be rubbed back and forth
so as to cover the whole length of the stone
to keep the surface flat. After a while however, the stone does wear hollow and it
must then be rubbed on a flat stone using
sand and water as an abrasive to get it flat
once more.

For the sharpening of curved edges
shaped oilstones, known as slips, are used.
These are also available in three grades,
fine, medium, and coarse, Fig. 132.

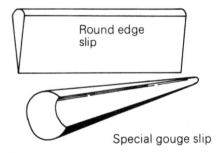

Fig. 132

Wood Rasps, Fig. 133

Use. For the shaping of difficult curves.

Parts. 1. Blade — hardened, and covered with teeth

2. Tang — softened, and tapered for a wooden handle.

The teeth of a rasp are not cut but are formed by squeezing the metal from in front.
The shape is known by the blade section and they are made flat, round and half-round.
The cabinet rasp is half-round but the blade is a little wider and thinner than the half-

Fig. 133   Cabinet rasp—half round

round wood rasp. Lengths vary from 150 mm to 400 mm, but 200 mm will be found quite suitable. Where possible, always use a cutting tool for wood, a rasp is an abrading tool and should only be used for awkward shapes where a cutting tool cannot be used.

Glass Paper

Use. For removing small defects on the wood surface.

Glasspaper is an abrasive, that is it scrapes away by rubbing. It is made in ten grades in sheets 280 mm by 230 mm. The pieces of ground glass are graded for size by the use of sieves and glued to a paper backing. For convenience, a sheet may be cut into six pieces, one piece is wrapped round a cork rubber and worked back and forth along the grain. The soft cork rubber ensures that the wood surface is not damaged. Never work right to the edges or they will lose their sharpness. For special shapes and curves, small rubbers to fit should be made from scrapwood.

Hardwood surfaces can be brought to a smooth glossy finish by the careful use of a piece of fine grade glasspaper after the wood has been cleaned off properly with the smoothing plane and scraper.

Where the wood is to be painted the surface should be left slightly rough by rubbing across the grain with a coarser grade of paper.

Garnet is a very hard natural abrasive graded and glued to paper 280 mm by 230 mm.

Garnet paper is coated both 'open' and 'closed'. In open paper, the abrasive grains are spaced apart so that the paper does not fill or choke when rubbing down paintwork or soft resinous woods. Close papers have the grain packed together to form a regular surface and are suitable for the rubbing of hard surfaces. Glasspaper has a closed coat.

The following table compares the grading of the two abrasives:

GRIT SIZE	GARNET CABINET PAPER		GARNET FINISHING PAPER	GLASSPAPER
	Closed	*Open*	*Open*	*Closed*
220	—	6/0	6/0	Flour
180	—	5/0	5/0	2/0
150	4/0	4/0	4/0	0
120	3/0	3/0	3/0	1
100	2/0	2/0	2/0	$1\frac{1}{2}$
80	0	0	0	F2 (Fine)
60	$\frac{1}{2}$	$\frac{1}{2}$	—	M2 (Middle)
50	1	1	—	S2 (Strong)
40	$1\frac{1}{2}$	$1\frac{1}{2}$	—	$2\frac{1}{2}$
36	2	2	—	3

The grit size number indicates the number of meshes per 25 mm length through which the grit will pass. 3/0 is a shortened way of writing 000.

For softwoods, M2, 1½, and 1 grades of glasspaper are suitable; while for hardwoods, F2, 1, and 0 are best, or their equivalent in Garnet paper.

Once, woodworkers made their own abrasive by sprinkling sand on glued paper. Although there is now no such thing as sandpaper it is still quite common in industry to speak of 'sanding' when using abrasive paper.

Exercises

1. Make a neat sketch of a firmer chisel and name five main parts.

2. Sketch and describe a registered pattern chisel.

3. How many types of gouges are there? Describe each kind.

4. The head of a mallet slides easily on its shaft. What prevents the head from flying off in use?

5. What precaution would you take to keep an oilstone in good condition?

6. What oil should be used on an oilstone?

7. Give at least two examples where a wood rasp could be used.

8. In what way do the teeth of a rasp differ from a file?

9. What is glasspaper? When would you use it? How would you use it?

10. Give one necessary safety precaution when using a chisel.

(EAST ANGLIAN REGIONAL EXAMINATIONS BOARD)

11. What is the lubricant used:
    (a) When grinding on a sandstone?
    (b) When finishing an edge on an oilstone?

(SOUTH-EAST REGIONAL EXAMINATIONS BOARD)

12. Why is a glasspaper block or glasspaper 'rubber' usually made of, or faced with, cork?

(WEST MIDLANDS EXAMINATIONS BOARD)

9
The Brace and Bit: Drills

Brace, Fig. 134

Use. For holding bits when boring and countersinking in wood.
Parts. 1. Head — hardwood, mounted in a ball bearing
2. Crank — steel
3. Handle — hardwood
4. Chuck — steel
5. 2 Jaws — steel

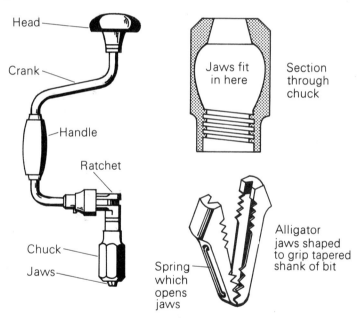

Fig. 134 Joiners' ratchet brace

The making of a hole using a brace and bit is known as boring, and is best done horizontally or vertically, Fig. 135. Where possible, bore horizontally for two reasons:
1. There is less danger of the work slipping in the vice when pushing against the vice jaws.

77

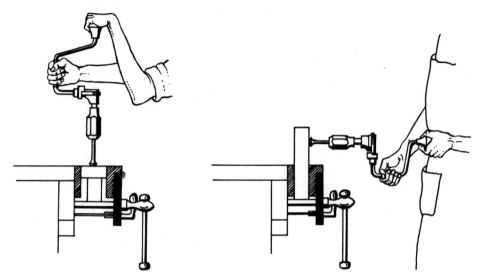

Fig. 135a   Vertical boring. Note the use of a
packing piece in the vice to prevent the work
slipping.

Fig. 135b   Horizontal boring. The work
pushes against the vice jaws and cannot slip.

2. More pressure can be applied to the
   brace with the body.

A ratchet brace is the better kind
because it enables us to work in corners
where a full turn on an ordinary brace
would be impossible. The size is known by
the sweep and varies from 200 mm to
350 mm, Fig. 136. A 250 mm sweep is
suitable for school use.

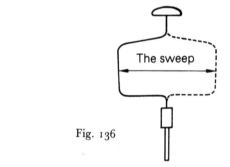

The sweep

Fig. 136

CENTRE BIT, old type, Fig. 137

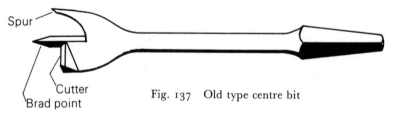

Spur

Cutter
Brad point

Fig. 137   Old type centre bit

Use. For the boring of shallow holes.

The centre bit is not suitable for the boring of deep holes because it tends to drift out
of line.

It is available in a wide range of sizes from 6 mm to 50 mm, this size being the diameter of the hole it will bore. These bits usually have a black finish but can be obtained bright.

CENTRE BIT, new pattern, Fig. 138

This is also used for the boring of shallow holes. The screw point draws the bit into the wood, while the cylindrical shape to the head reduces the tendency to drift out of line. Notice how a bit is sharpened, Fig. 139.

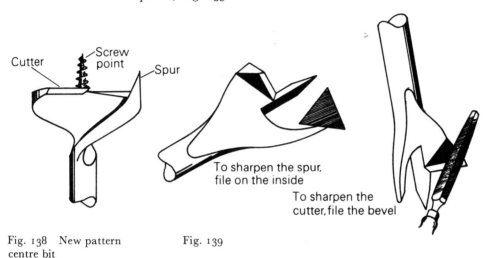

Fig. 138   New pattern centre bit

Fig. 139

AUGER BIT, Jennings pattern, Fig. 140

Fig. 140   Jennings pattern auger bit. The Jennings pattern dowel bit is similar but much shorter and precision ground to the diameter

Use. For the boring of deep holes in softwood and mild hardwoods.

The twisted body serves two purposes:
1. The outside diameter acts as a guide to the bit and prevents it drifting out of line.
2. The flutes enable the waste wood to escape.

The stages in boring a hole in wood are shown in Fig. 141.

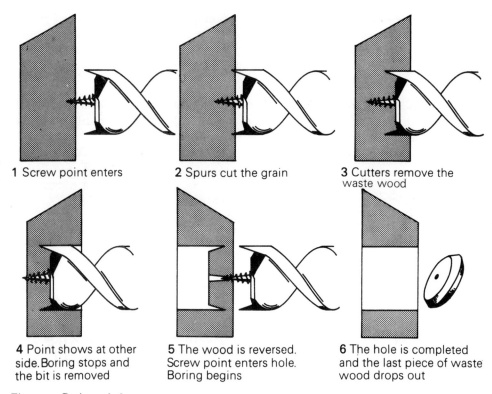

1 Screw point enters

2 Spurs cut the grain

3 Cutters remove the waste wood

4 Point shows at other side. Boring stops and the bit is removed

5 The wood is reversed. Screw point enters hole. Boring begins

6 The hole is completed and the last piece of waste wood drops out

Fig. 141   Boring a hole

FORSTNER PATTERN BIT, Fig. 142

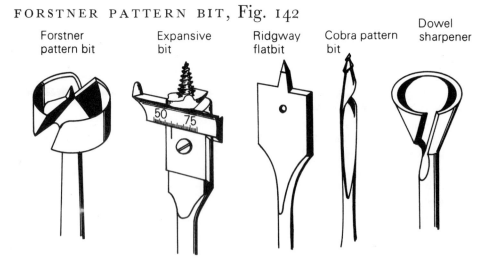

Forstner pattern bit

Expansive bit

Ridgway flatbit

Cobra pattern bit

Dowel sharpener

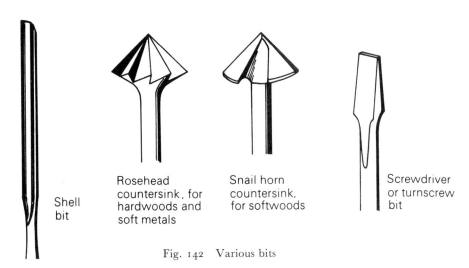

Shell bit

Rosehead countersink, for hardwoods and soft metals

Snail horn countersink, for softwoods

Screwdriver or turnscrew bit

Fig. 142   Various bits

Unlike other bits, the Forstner pattern bit is guided by its circular rim and not by the centre point. The holes bored are clean, true and flat bottomed and can be overlapped without difficulty. In use, it is unaffected by knots or variations in the grain. It is ideal for making recesses as when making a box for the oilstone and is popular with cabinet makers for all kinds of exacting work.

EXPANSIVE BIT

This tool is used for the boring of large shallow holes especially in softwood. Being adjustable for different sizes it saves the expense of buying a number of large diameter bits.

Expansive bits are made in two sizes:

Small, with two cutters Nos. 1 and 2 to cut a range of holes from 13 mm to 38 mm diameter, and

Large, with two cutters Nos. 3 and 4 to cut a range of holes from 22 mm to 75 mm.

Extra cutters are available for the large bit enabling it to cut holes up to 150 mm diameter. A scale of hole diameters is marked on the cutter which is set to a witness mark on the bit and locked in position by a screw.

FLATBITS

This boring tool has an unusual design in that the cutting edge extends from the point, along the edges to the sides. The holes are bored cleanly and the flatbit is ideal for use in electric drills where high speeds are obtainable.

COBRA PATTERN BIT

For boring small holes to take wood screws and nails. The sizes range from No. 2 to 12, the number indicating the size of the bit in 0·8 mm.

SHELL BIT

For boring clean small holes such as those required for screws.

ROSEHEAD COUNTERSINK

For opening out the end of a hole to take the head of a countersunk screw. This pattern is intended for hardwoods and non-ferrous metals.

SNAIL HORN COUNTERSINK

This has a cone-shaped nose with one or two cutters and should ONLY be used on soft-woods.

DOWEL SHARPENER

This is used for chamfering the ends of a dowel so that it will enter its hole easily. The tool has one cutter and is 19 mm diameter at the mouth. Compare it with the snailhorn countersink.

SCREWDRIVER BIT

The great advantage in using the brace is the leverage. This enables screws to be properly tightened or removed with little effort. There is little leverage on an ordinary screw-driver and much of its power comes from its length which stores energy when twisted in use.

Bradawl, Fig. 143

The bradawl in use. Push the blade in the wood across the grain, then twist back and forth.

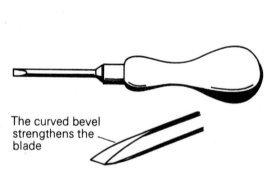

The curved bevel strengthens the blade

Fig. 143 Bradawl

Fig. 144

Use. For making small holes for nails and screws.

Parts. 1. Blade — hardened steel

2. Hardwood handle — ash or beech

The bradawl blade must be kept sharp by rubbing both sides of the bevel on the oilstone. To make a hole, press the blade into the wood with the edge across the grain then slightly rotate the tool in both directions. The action of pushing and twisting continues until the hole is the correct depth, Fig. 144.

Bradawls are made in six sizes, from No. 1 to No. 6, and can be obtained with the blade pinned to the handle. This is done to prevent the handle coming off when withdrawing the tool from a deep hole.

Hand Drill, Fig. 145

Use. For holding straight shank twist drills for the drilling of holes.

Parts. 1. Frame — malleable iron

2. Gear wheel — cast iron

3. Pinions — cast iron

4. Chuck — steel

5. 3 Jaws — steel

6. Handles — beech

This is a handy tool for the accurate drilling of small holes suitable for nails and screws. The chuck capacity is 8 mm.

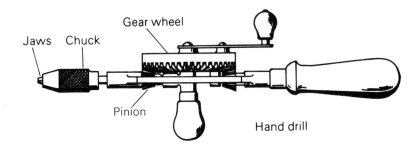

Fig. 145

TWIST DRILL, Fig. 146

Use. For use with the hand drill.

A set of twist drills from 1.5 mm to 7.5 mm by 0.5 mm is sufficient for general work though a full set up to 10.5 mm and mounted in a stand is better if a power drilling machine is available.

Warning: DO NOT use a screw-point bit in a power tool.

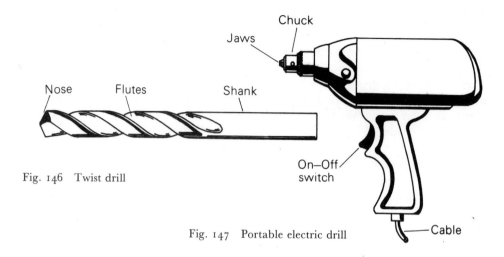

Fig. 146   Twist drill

Fig. 147   Portable electric drill

Portable Electric Drill, Fig. 147

The most useful size of portable drill is the 6 mm which means it will take drills up to 6 mm diameter. This power tool is light to hold and easy to carry about, the larger sizes being too heavy for school use.

The tool consists of an electric motor, geared to a small chuck, and a handle for holding, which includes a trigger switch for starting and stopping the motor. Electricity is very useful but can be dangerous, so if you notice any wear on the cable, plug, or drill report it at once to your teacher. Electricity is always seeking the quickest way to earth and for this reason the metal body of the tool is 'earthed' in case of accidents. This means that if something goes wrong the electricity will not harm you. Even though all this care has been taken, be sensible when handling these power tools and remember the following:

1. Work as near the wall plug as possible to avoid long lengths of trailing cable in the room.
2. Do not stand in water or on damp ground.
3. Do not stand on concrete — it is always damp, use wood or a rubber mat.
4. Wear rubber soled shoes and rubber gloves.
5. Be wise! Do not let electricity take a short cut to earth through you!

Exercises

1. Make a neat sketch of three of the following, and state the purpose for which you would use each:
   (a) centre bit; (b) auger bit; (c) dowel bit; (d) Forstner pattern bit; (e) snailhorn countersink; (f) dowel rounder.

2. Make a neat sketch of a bradawl. Describe clearly how it should be used and for what purpose.

3. State three precautions when using portable electric drills.

4. For what purpose would you use a hand drill?

5. Explain, step by step, how you would bore a 19 mm diameter hole right through a 25 mm thick piece of softwood.

6. Why is it dangerous to use a screw-point bit in an electric drill?

7. Make a neat sketch of a centre bit. Label the three main parts at the cutting end, and state the purpose of each.

8. Which bit would you choose to bore a 13 mm diameter hole 75 mm deep in the edge of a pine board? Give reasons for your choice.

10

Glues and Fixing Devices

Glues

There is a wide variety of glues from which to choose so care must be taken to select the best one for the job.

ANIMAL GLUES

These low priced glues are made mainly from various parts of the bodies of cattle. They are available in loose form as well as in tubes and tins, some of which can be used cold, others hot. Their strength is excellent, they do not stain the wood and are easy to prepare, though hot glues should be used in a warm room to prevent them chilling. Animal glues are neither heatproof nor waterproof.

Scotch glue is a popular kind and is made from the bones and hides of cattle. The bones are cleaned, broken, and washed to remove grease and then polished. In this clean state they are placed in special ovens where hot water and steam act on them to produce a weak liquid glue. This is concentrated to bring it to the required strength, defoaming agents and preservatives are added and the glue is poured into trays. When cool, the glue is cut into slices, called cakes, which are dried on wire netting shelves in tunnels of warm air. These netting marks can be clearly seen on the glue cakes, Fig. 148. The glue is also available in the form of small pellets known as pearl glue which is made by rapidly chilling glue droplets. Animal glues are nowadays usually ground and sold in powder form.

The production of hide glue is similar but, having a high strength when first made, it needs less concentrating. Scotch glue is dark brown in colour, but a thinner amber-coloured cake is available known as French glue.

A piece of animal glue should feel sticky when rubbed with a damp finger, it should be clear when seen against the light and there should be no unpleasant smell.

To prepare Scotch glue:

1. Break a cake of glue into small pieces. This is best done by wrapping it in cloth to prevent the pieces flying about when hammered.
2. Soak the pieces in a jar of water for several hours to form a jelly, Fig. 149.
3. Place the jelly with a little water in the inner pot of a glue kettle, Fig. 150.
4. Half fill the outer pot with clean water and heat slowly.
   If using a powdered or jelly form stages 1 and 2 are omitted.

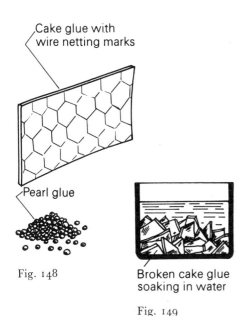

Cake glue with wire netting marks

Pearl glue

Fig. 148

Broken cake glue soaking in water

Fig. 149

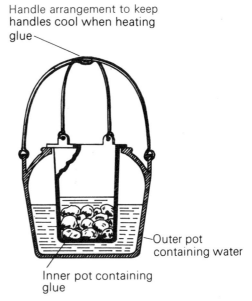

Handle arrangement to keep handles cool when heating glue

Outer pot containing water

Inner pot containing glue

Fig. 150   Glue pot

The boiling water in the outer pot will melt the glue without burning it. A thin skin forms when the glue is ready and this must be removed with a piece of wood. The correct strength is when the glue runs off the brush in a steady stream and if it does not, more water or glue must be added, Fig. 151. Unless large joints are being glued, the normal glue brush is too big. For small joints, the glue is best applied with a small strip of wood. Keep the glue pot clean and well tinned and avoid all iron contamination.

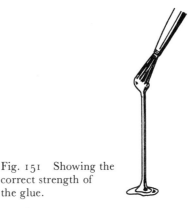

Fig. 151   Showing the correct strength of the glue.

GLUING

The parts to be glued should be clean and well fitting. Each part should be given a thin coating of glue, squeezed together as quickly as possible and held with a cramp until the glue has set hard. Best results are obtained with the glue at a temperature of 49 °C in a room at 21 °C.

CASEIN GLUE

This is prepared by mixing a powder with cold water. The powder is made from skimmed milk 33 500 l of milk being required to produce 1 tonne of casein. The glue is popular for joinery work where large surfaces have to be joined such as in the making of flush doors and the laying of laminated plastic sheets. They are moderately heat and waterproof but tend to stain hardwoods. Setting depends partly on chemical action so casein glue cannot be used for making rubbed joints.

SYNTHETIC RESIN GLUES

These are made in two parts, the actual resinous glue and the hardener. The glue is normally in the form of a syrup but only has a storage life of several months because the chemical action which turns it into a hard resin cannot be completely stopped. In use, the syrup is smeared over one part of the joint and the hardener over the other, the joint is assembled and chemical action quickly sets the glue hard. Different hardeners or accelerators are available to give different setting speeds, though a warm room or hot press shortens the hardening time.

The glue is also made in powder form and is prepared by first mixing it to a thin paste by the addition of water. As before, the hardener is separate. To simplify the handling of this glue still further it is made in powder form complete with the hardener. Once mixed with water to a paste, hardening begins, so only enough should be prepared for immediate use. Joints should be a good fit otherwise the glue will crack and turn to powder in the spaces. Special gap-filling hardeners can be obtained to reduce crazing in loose-fitting joints.

A different type of synthetic resin glue is the emulsion. This is a creamy white fluid, clean, easy to use and does not stain the wood. There is no hardener. The emulsion is applied cold, usually to one part of the joint only which must be assembled while the glue is still in a position to wet thoroughly the second surface. At a normal workshop temperature of 20 °C the glue will take 20 hours to set though considerable strength will have been reached in 1 hour. A cold room will slow down the setting time as emulsions set solely by absorption/evaporation of the water.

CONTACT GLUES

These are based on synthetic rubbers and resins in a solvent. As rubber is a very flexible and elastic material this type has little strength but is most satisfactory for holding sheets of light material in place in cool, dry conditions. Adhesion results because two dry films of rubber or synthetic rubber will unite under slight pressure. For this reason contact or 'impact' adhesives are used where pressure is difficult to apply to light panels.

In use, the glue is spread over both surfaces, a metal comb being used to ensure an even film. After 15 minutes to allow the solvent to evaporate, the two surfaces are brought together when 'grab' is immediate. Care must be taken to get one end of the panel correctly positioned after which it can be laid flat on the base, pressing from the centre outwards to avoid trapping air. Once the two surfaces grab, they cannot be separated. This glue tends to stain hardwood.

After all gluing operations the hands should be well washed. Casein and synthetic resin glues can cause a rash to form on the hands.

Hammers

WARRINGTON PATTERN HAMMER, Fig. 152

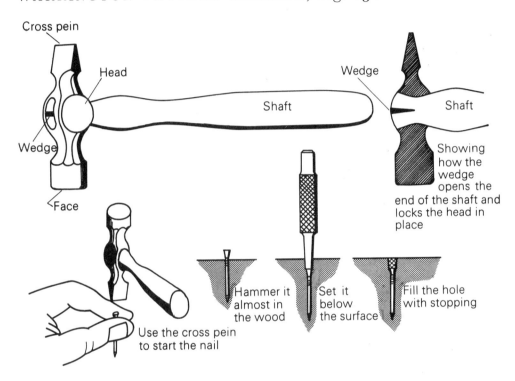

Fig. 152   Warrington hammer

Use.   For light nailing in cabinet work.
Parts.   1. Head — hardened steel
      2. Shaft — ash or hickory
      3. Wedges — wood and metal
Sizes are as follows:

NO.	00	0	1	2	3	4
APPROX. WEIGHT OF HEAD (GRAMMES)	170	230	280	340	400	450

ADZE EYE CLAW HAMMER, Fig. 153

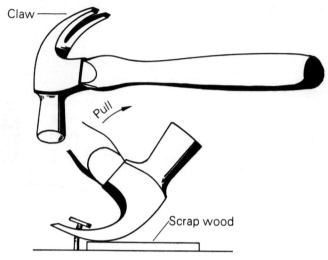

Fig. 153 Adze eye claw hammer

Use. For heavy nailing in carpentry work.

This hammer is heavier than the Warrington pattern and the claw is used for levering wire nails out of timber.

Sizes are:

NO.	I	2	3	4
APPROX. WEIGHT OF HEAD (GRAMMES)	370	450	570	680

Pincers, Fig. 154

Use. For levering small nails out of wood.

Tower pincers are the most suitable for woodworkers. The jaws are rounded so that having gripped the nail the tool can be rolled over to use leverage to withdraw it. One handle ends in a ball for safe handling and the other has a small claw for removing tacks and prising in general.

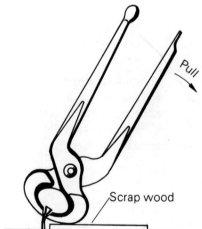

Fig. 154 Pincers in use

Nail sets or Punches, Fig. 155

Use. For punching or setting nail heads
below the surface of wood.

They are made of tool steel, with a
hardened point and are available from
1.5 mm to 5 mm, the smaller sizes being
the most useful for panel pins.

Nails, Fig. 156

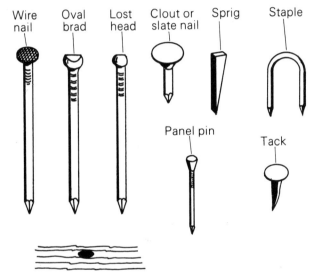

Fig. 155 Nail
set, showing
domed point to
fit the nail
head

Using oval nails: the longest axis
of the shape should follow the
grain to prevent splitting the wood

Fig. 156 Nails

Nails are made in different lengths, shapes, and sizes, and are used for quickly fixing
together wood as well as joining fibreboard and roofing felt to wooden parts. Nails are
usually made from steel wire and may be plated to prevent rusting. For a strong joint
the nails should be driven in at a slight angle called dovetailing, but they must be
staggered along the length of the wood to avoid splitting the grain, Fig. 157. To get a
secure grip the nail length should be three times the thickness of the wood being held
though longer nails must be used when nailing onto end grain. When nailing near the
end of a length of wood a small hole should be bored to prevent the grain splitting. This
hole must be a little smaller than the nail diameter to allow for gripping. Blunting the
nail point with a hammer also prevents splitting the wood. When ordering nails state:

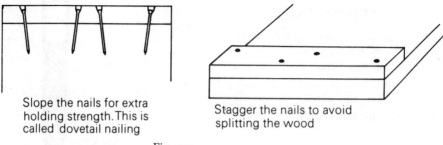

Slope the nails for extra
holding strength. This is
called dovetail nailing

Stagger the nails to avoid
splitting the wood

Fig. 157

1. Quantity by weight
2. Type
3. Finish
4. Length and diameter

e.g., 1 Kg steel, round, lost head nails, 38 mm × 14 g.

ROUND PLAIN-HEAD WIRE NAILS

These are made from 13 mm to 250 mm long, with flat heads ridged to prevent the hammer slipping off. The neck is also ridged to grip the wood better. Wire nails have good gripping qualities and should be driven in straight to let their flat heads lie on the wood surface. They are used in carpentry, packing case manufacture, and any rough work where the appearance of large nail heads is unimportant.

OVAL BRAD-HEAD NAILS

The shank of these nails is elliptical not oval, and when nailing, the longer axis should be in line with the grain to prevent splitting. The holding power is not so great as the round wire nails but the small head can be punched below the wood surface and the hole stopped to make a neater job.

LOST HEAD NAILS, Oval and round.

These are similar to the oval brad but have a smaller head and are available with either a round or elliptical sectioned shank. The nail head is easily 'lost' or punched below the wood surface.

CLOUT OR SLATE NAIL

A large-headed nail suitable for fixing soft material to wood. A clout nail with an extra large head is available for fixing roofing felt and should, of course, be galvanized.

PANEL PIN

This is a thin nail with a tapered head popular with cabinet makers because the head is easily concealed. The sizes range from 13 mm to 75 mm in gauges from 20 to 12.

TACK

A short steel nail with a large head and is either blued or tinned to prevent rusting. It is used in upholstery work for securing soft materials, such as webbing, to the wooden framework.

SPRIG

A headless tapered nail for securing the backs of pictures and window panes in their frames. When fixing window panes a short length of matchstick should be placed between the sprig and the glass to prevent breakage.

STAPLE

A U-shaped nail for securing wire netting to wood and holding small cables and cord in place.

Screwdrivers, Fig. 158

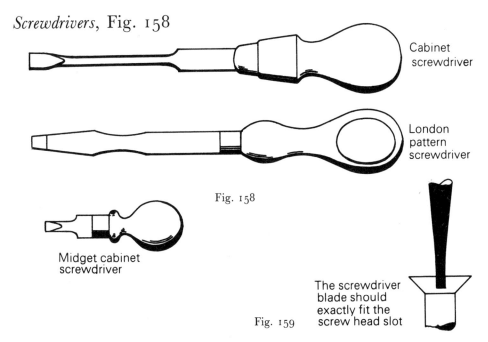

Cabinet screwdriver

London pattern screwdriver

Fig. 158

Midget cabinet screwdriver

The screwdriver blade should exactly fit the screw head slot

Fig. 159

Use. For fixing and removing wood screws.

The screwdriver blade is made of hardened steel and mounted in a wood or plastic handle. Many patterns are available in different sizes and it is important to have several, each ground to accurately fit a different size of wood screw slot, Fig. 159.

PHILLIPS SCREWDRIVER, Fig. 160

This has been developed to produce a better-fitting driver and screw. The screw head has a recessed slot of cross shape into which the special blade fits. The blade is made in four sizes and two grades, 'H' indicating a hard blade for use with self-tapping screws, and 'N' a normal blade for general wood screw use.

The Phillips method of screw fixing has been further developed resulting in a more detailed recess in the screw head. This is called the Pozidriv and has, of course, a special blade to suit, Fig. 161. In an emergency, the Phillips driver will fit a pozidriv screw but the pozidriv will not fit a Phillips screw. The main advantage of the Phillips and pozidriv methods is that the better fitting blades do not 'cam-out' or ride out of the slots causing damage to the screw heads.

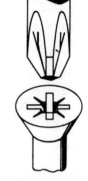

Fig. 160 Phillips screw and driver

Fig. 161 Pozidriv screw and driver

The sizes are as follows:

SCREWDRIVER SIZE NO.	FOR SCREW GAUGE NO.
1	3–4
2	5–10
3	12–14
4	15 and over

Wood Screws

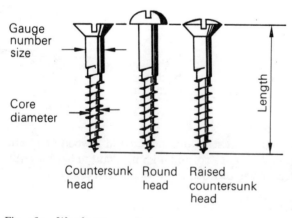

Gauge number size

Core diameter

Length

Countersunk head

Round head

Raised countersunk head

Fig. 162 Wood screws

Screw cup. For use where appearance is important or where the screw must be removed frequently

Fig. 163

Use. 1. For the temporary fixing of wood and metal fittings.

2. For an accurate, neat, and strong method of fastening parts together.

Parts. 1. Head

2. Shank

3. Thread

Screw heads are made in three shapes, round, countersunk, and raised countersunk, Fig. 162. The countersunk is used where there must be no projections, the raised countersunk has a better appearance and, if often removed from the wood, is used with a cup to protect the countersink hole from damage, Fig. 163.

The round head is actually a semi-ellipse in section and is used where a part to be joined is too thin for countersinking, such as in metal brackets.

The size of a screw is the diameter of the shank which is known by a gauge number, the larger the number the larger the shank diameter. Numbers 4, 6, 8, and 10 are the popular sizes.

The length of thread is twice the length of the shank so where possible use a screw length three times the thickness of the wood being held.

Wood screws are made of different metals such as steel and brass and may be left natural or coated with metal or painted for protection.

FITTING A WOOD SCREW, Fig. 164

1 Bore a clearance hole for the screw shank   **2** Bore a hole the size of the screw core   **3** Countersink if required   **4** Wax the end of the screw thread and drive in the screw

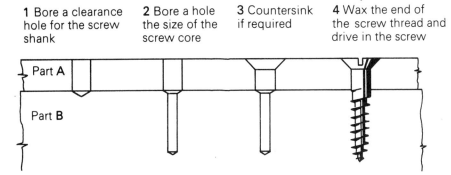

Fig. 164   Fitting a wood screw

Two holes must always be drilled, one to clear the shank and one to clear the core. This allows the screw to cut its own thread in the wood. Always use a little soap or wax on the end of the thread not only to make cutting easier but to protect the screw from the chemicals in the wood and make removal easier at some later date. Oak contains tannic acid and when this comes in contact with iron and steel, ink is formed, the amount depending on the dampness of the wood. Where steel screws have been used on oak doors one can usually see these dark blue stains, and in time the screws will be destroyed and the door will fall off. On small work, brass screws must be used in oak but because these are soft and easily broken a steel screw of similar size should be used first to cut the thread. For heavy work, plated screws are available as well as stainless steel screws which are about six times the price of the ordinary steel type.

When ordering wood screws state:

1. Material
2. Style of head and whether slotted or recessed
3. Length and diameter (in screw gauge number)
4. Details of plating if required.

e.g. Steel, slotted c's'k head wood screws, 38·1 mm × 8 s.g. (Countersunk is usually abbreviated to 'csk'.)

Exercises

1. Name a resin glue with which you have had some experience. State how it was prepared for use, the joint for which it was used, and any precautions that were necessary during and after gluing.

2. What is a contact glue? Describe a piece of work where it could be used.

3. Make a neat sketch of a Warrington hammer. Show how the head is secured to the shaft.

4. Name the glue you would consider to be most suited for the following purposes:
   (a) making a rubbed joint between two long boards to form a table-top,
   (b) applying a sheet of Formica to a fitted kitchen working surface, so situated that no pressure can be applied to assist in the adhesion,
   (c) gluing a brass tube into a hole bored in a wooden table lamp base,
   (d) gluing together several veneers between curved formers to make laminated ribs for a canoe. (MIDDLESEX REGIONAL EXAMINING BOARD)

5. Nails and screws are methods of fastening pieces of wood together. Explain in detail, with sketches, ONE example of the use of EACH. (EAST MIDLAND REGIONAL EXAMINATIONS BOARD)

6. Make a good clear sketch of a pair of pincers. Explain how their special shape enables them to work efficiently. Describe the most effective method of removing a nail with the pincers. (ASSOCIATED LANCASHIRE SCHOOLS EXAMINING BOARD)

7. Nailing, screwing, and gluing are different methods of holding two pieces of wood together; give example in which each is most suitably employed. (WEST MIDLANDS EXAMINATIONS BOARD)

8. Make a sketch to show what is meant by 'dovetail' nailing. Why is this done? (WEST MIDLANDS EXAMINATIONS BOARD)

9. Screws can be obtained with various shaped heads. Sketch and name three types of screw heads and give an example where each type could be used. Under what circumstances would you use brass screws in preference to steel screws?

Explain, with the aid of sketches, how you would insert 38·1 mm brass screws to hold together two pieces of hardwood each 25 mm thick. (SOUTHERN REGIONAL EXAMINATIONS BOARD)

I I

Joints and their Use

There are three basic forms of construction in woodwork, Fig. 165:
  Box or carcase
  Frame
  Stool

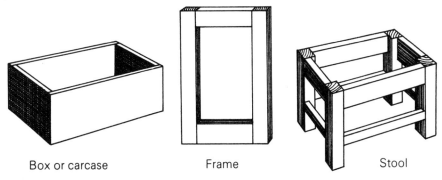

Box or carcase   Frame   Stool

Fig. 165   Forms of construction

Box construction includes boxes of all kinds, cabinets, bedside lockers, and bookcases. The joints used are:
  Butt
  Corner rebate
  Housing
  Box dovetail
Frame construction includes door, mirror and window frames. The joints used are:
  Halving
  Bridle
  Dowelled
  Mortice and tenon
Stool construction includes stools, chairs, tables, and tea trolleys. The joints used are:
  Dowelled
  Mortice and tenon
  Where parts of a job, such as the sides, are identical they are held together in the vice or clamped so that all lengths can be marked along their edges in one operation. This is

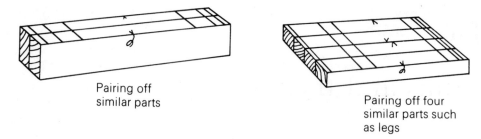

Pairing off
similar parts

Pairing off four
similar parts such
as legs

Fig. 166

called pairing off and ensures that the opposite sides are exactly the same length, Fig. 166. After unclamping, the marks are squared all round each piece of wood.

When making a box, stool, or frame, the parts forming the sides should be placed flat on the bench and their ends numbered to avoid confusion when joint-making, and to ensure correct assembly, Fig. 167. After cutting the joints, all inside surfaces should be cleaned up with the smoothing plane, scraped if the material is hardwood, and glass-papered to a good finish. The work is glued together, cramped and tested for squareness by testing the lengths of the two diagonals with a narrow strip of wood. The work is square when the two diagonals are the same length, Fig. 168. After the glue has set hard, the outside of the work is cleaned up, just as the inside was, then the job is ready for the finishing treatment.

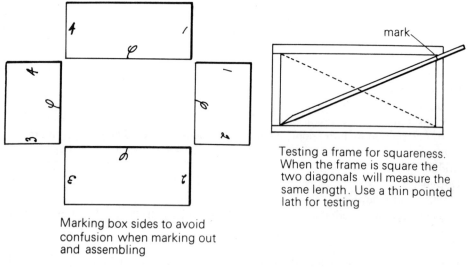

mark

Testing a frame for squareness.
When the frame is square the
two diagonals will measure the
same length. Use a thin pointed
lath for testing

Marking box sides to avoid
confusion when marking out
and assembling

Fig. 167

Fig. 168

Joints
BUTT, Fig. 169

This corner joint has a small gluing area, no shoulders to assist accurate assembly and is weak. The end grain absorbs much of the glue and the nails do not hold very well in end grain.

CORNER REBATE, Fig. 170

A stronger and easily made joint. Notice from which side the nails are driven. The steps in making the corner rebate are shown in Fig. 171.

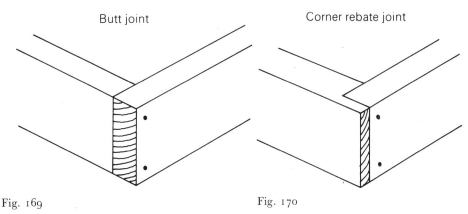

Butt joint   Corner rebate joint

Fig. 169   Fig. 170

Making a corner rebate joint

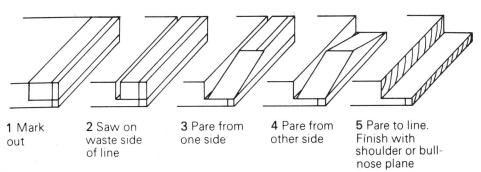

1 Mark out   **2** Saw on waste side of line   **3** Pare from one side   **4** Pare from other side   **5** Pare to line. Finish with shoulder or bull-nose plane

Fig. 171

HOUSING, Fig. 172

The through housing is suitable for unimportant work or work which is to be painted. After marking out, the groove is sawn to the line and the waste wood pared out from both sides. Where appearance is important as in, say, bookshelves, the front of the joint

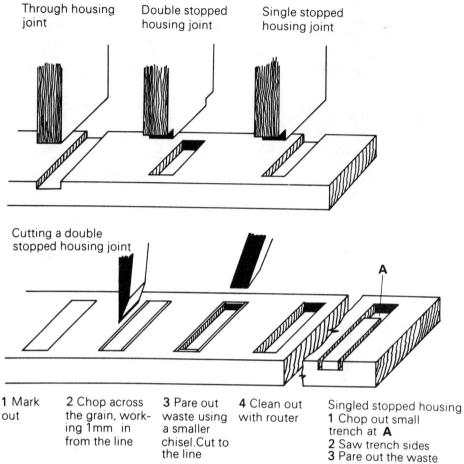

Through housing joint

Double stopped housing joint

Single stopped housing joint

Cutting a double stopped housing joint

1 Mark out

2 Chop across the grain, working 1mm in from the line

3 Pare out waste using a smaller chisel.Cut to the line

4 Clean out with router

Singled stopped housing
1 Chop out small trench at **A**
2 Saw trench sides
3 Pare out the waste

Fig. 172   The housing joint

is stopped to preserve the straight line of the wood. Before the saw can be used, a small space must be chopped out at the stopped end after which the groove is sawn and chiselled to the line. When the work is seen from both sides the joint is stopped at both ends and the groove must be chopped out with the chisel.

BOX OR THROUGH DOVETAIL

This is the strongest corner joint and is made by cutting dovetails on one piece of wood and pins on the other so that when assembled the joints lock together in one direction. When marking out it is important to see that this locking action operates in the correct direction, for example with a portable case or box, the base should be held by the sides, Fig. 173. Where this is unimportant, it is usual to place the tails on the longer pieces.

For maximum strength tails and pins should be the same thickness as the wood, but for appearance, the joint looks better if the tails are much longer and the pins shorter, Fig. 174.

The dovetail slope is one in eight for hardwoods and one in six for softwoods, and gives reasonable strength without risk of the grain crumbling, Fig. 175. The joint can be made by cutting first either the pins or the tails, there is no agreement among wood-workers about this. In the method shown, the tails are cut first, Fig. 176.

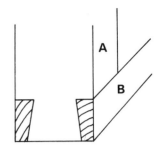

Piece **A** is holding piece **B**

Fig. 173   The dovetail joint

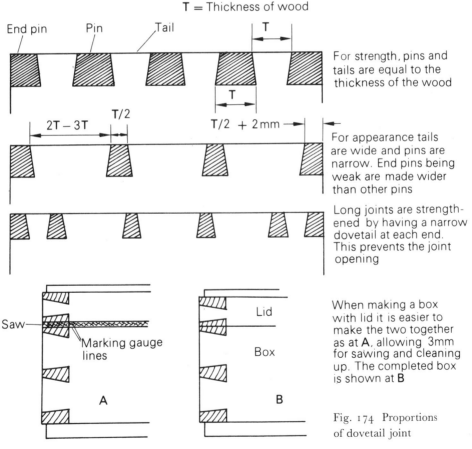

T = Thickness of wood

End pin   Pin   Tail   T

For strength, pins and tails are equal to the thickness of the wood

2T – 3T   T/2   T/2 + 2mm

For appearance tails are wide and pins are narrow. End pins being weak are made wider than other pins

Long joints are strength-ened by having a narrow dovetail at each end. This prevents the joint opening

Saw   Marking gauge lines   A

Lid   Box   B

When making a box with lid it is easier to make the two together as at **A**, allowing 3mm for sawing and cleaning up. The completed box is shown at **B**

Fig. 174 Proportions of dovetail joint

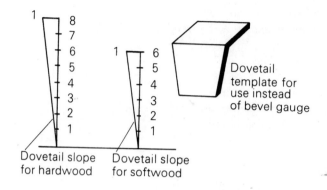

Dovetail
template for
use instead
of bevel gauge

Dovetail slope
for hardwood

Dovetail slope
for softwood

Fig. 175

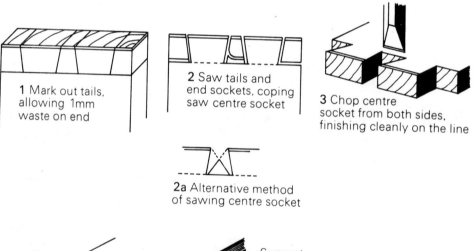

1 Mark out tails,
allowing 1mm
waste on end

2 Saw tails and
end sockets, coping
saw centre socket

3 Chop centre
socket from both sides,
finishing cleanly on the line

2a Alternative method
of sawing centre socket

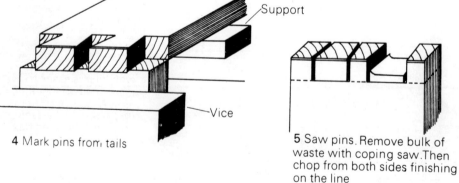

Support

Vice

4 Mark pins from tails

5 Saw pins. Remove bulk of
waste with coping saw. Then
chop from both sides finishing
on the line

Fig. 176   Making a dovetail joint

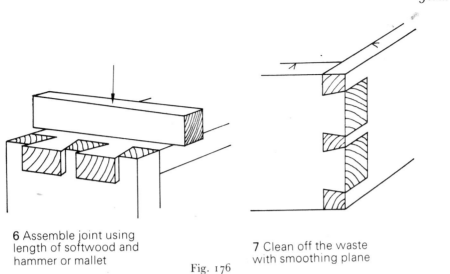

6 Assemble joint using
length of softwood and
hammer or mallet

Fig. 176

7 Clean off the waste
with smoothing plane

CROSS HALVING, Fig. 177

Notice how the joint is marked out so that when assembled the face edge marks are on
the same side of the completed work.

Cross halving joint marked out.

Pencil lines shown dotted, cut
lines full. Wastewood is shaded

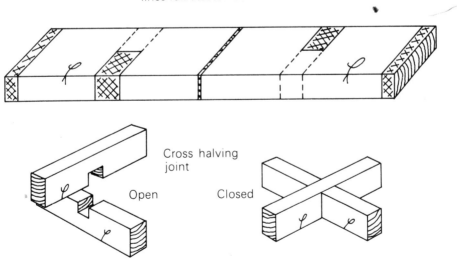

Cross halving
joint

Open   Closed

Fig. 177

CORNER, T, AND DOVETAIL HALVING, Fig. 178

In each of these joints, both pieces of wood are marked to half their thickness using the marking gauge from the face side. The corner halving is cut completely with the saw, first along the grain, then across. This joint is usually assembled with nails or screws. The dovetail and T-halving joints are cut with saw and chisel. When marking out the dovetail, allow 3 mm waste at each edge to start the saw.

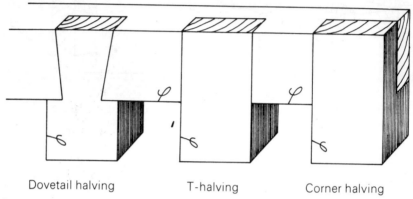

Dovetail halving   T-halving   Corner halving

Fig. 178

DOWELLED JOINT, Fig. 179

A dowel is a cylindrical hardwood pin, usually made of beech, and must be straight and

1 Marked out   **2** Holes bored and dowels fitted

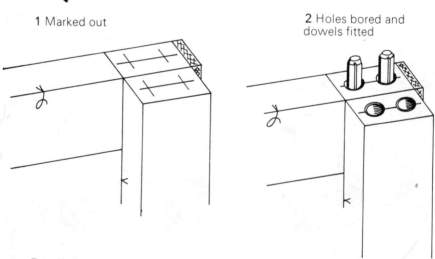

Fig. 179   Dowelled corner joint

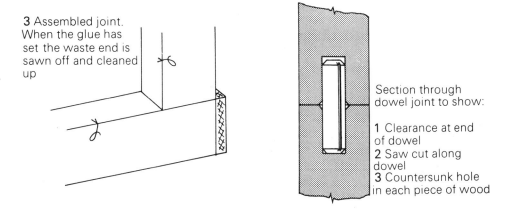

3 Assembled joint.
When the glue has
set the waste end is
sawn off and cleaned
up

Section through
dowel joint to show:

1 Clearance at end
of dowel
2 Saw cut along
dowel
3 Countersunk hole
in each piece of wood

Fig. 179   Dowel corner joint untrimmed

true for an accurate joint. Dowels are commonly used in chair-making, but they are also used in frame construction in general and the jointing of boards. At least two dowels should be used to prevent twisting, and where a number of joints are required a template saves much time when marking out.

Note:

1. The dowel ends must be chamfered with a dowel sharpener so that they will enter their holes easily.
2. A saw kerf must be made along the dowel length to allow trapped air and glue to escape.
3. The holes in the wood must be countersunk to allow for any wood swelling due to the tight fit of the dowel.
4. The dowels should be about 3 mm shorter than the combined depth of both holes to ensure that the joint closes tightly.

BRIDLE JOINT, Fig. 180

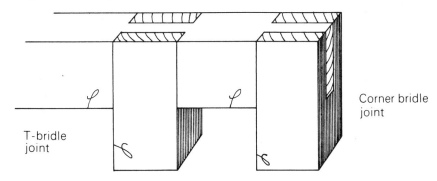

Corner bridle
joint

T-bridle
joint

Fig. 180

For maximum strength, the thickness of the wood is divided into three parts, as near equal as possible, and marked out with a mortice gauge. The joint is cut with a saw and chisel though a brace and bit could be used to remove most of the waste wood from the vertical pieces.

MORTICE AND TENON JOINT, Fig. 181

This is a very important joint in woodwork. It is widely used and there are many variations of it, depending on the type of construction and purpose of the work. The joint consists of a mortice, or slot, into which fits a tenon or tongue. Good proportions for a popular form of this joint are shown in Fig. 182.

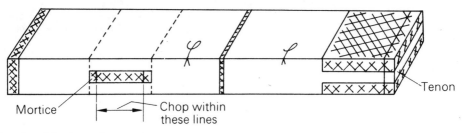

Fig. 181   Mortice and tenon joint marked out. Pencil lines shown dotted, cut lines full. Wastewood is shaded

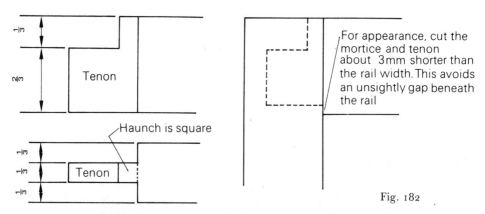

Fig. 182

    The mortice chisel is selected and should be as near as possible one-third of the wood thickness. The mortice gauge is set to the chisel and the joint marked out. To chop the mortice, the work should be placed on a flat piece of wood and cramped to the bench top or firmly held in the vice. By standing at the end of the work the chisel can be held vertically more easily as chopping proceeds.

Note: The widespread use of this joint has resulted in many different ways of its being made. For example, the bulk of the waste can be removed with the brace and bit, or chopping can begin in the middle of the mortice. Whatever method is used, success

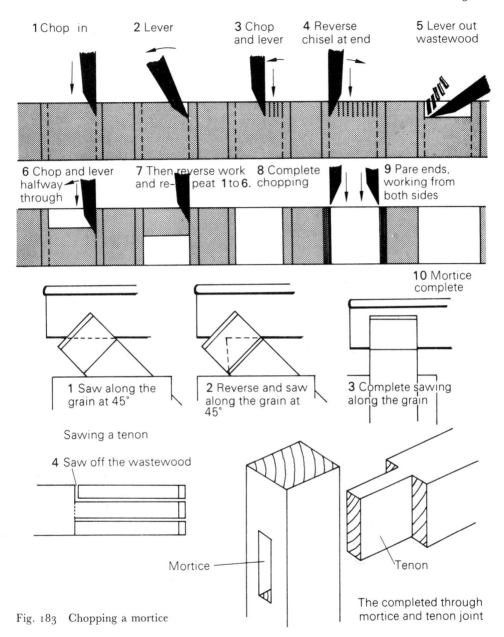

1 Chop in   2 Lever   3 Chop and lever   4 Reverse chisel at end   5 Lever out wastewood

6 Chop and lever halfway through   7 Then reverse work and re-peat 1 to 6.   8 Complete chopping   9 Pare ends, working from both sides

10 Mortice complete

1 Saw along the grain at 45°   2 Reverse and saw along the grain at 45°   3 Complete sawing along the grain

Sawing a tenon

4 Saw off the wastewood

Mortice

Tenon

The completed through mortice and tenon joint

Fig. 183   Chopping a mortice

depends upon accurate marking out, keeping the tools perfectly square to the work, chopping out exactly between the gauged lines, and accurately sawing the tenon, Fig. 183. The parts of a well made joint should slide together firmly but easily, the rough

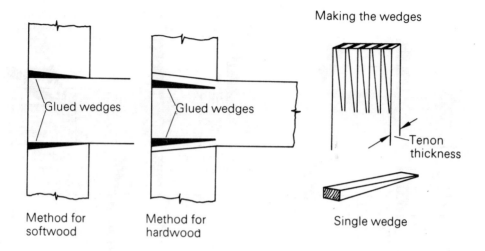

Making the wedges

Glued wedges

Glued wedges

Tenon thickness

Method for softwood

Method for hardwood

Single wedge

The ends of the mortice are tapered and the wedges driven in spaces to avoid splitting the softwood tenon. In hardwood, saw cuts are made nearly the length of the tenon and wedges driven in to give a dovetail effect

Fig. 184

surfaces from the saw making for a well glued joint. Figure 184 shows the wedged mortice and tenon.

STUB TENON, Fig. 185
When the tenon does not pass completely through the wood it is called a stub tenon and is generally used with a stopped mortice which is not cut right through the wood.

BAREFACED TENON, Fig. 186
A tenon having only one shoulder.

HAUNCHED MORTICE AND TENON JOINT, Fig. 187
When the mortice and tenon joint is made at a corner the mortice has to be shortened to keep it enclosed. This means that the tenon must be cut to suit. To prevent the outer or top part of the rail warping, a small square stub of the tenon is left which fits in the stile, and is called a square haunch. Where it is required to conceal a square haunch, as on some stools, the haunch is tapered and called a secret haunch.

GROOVED MORTICE AND TENON JOINT, Fig. 188
This joint is used in frames which are to hold unbreakable panels, usually of wood. The groove is one-third the thickness of the wood and as deep as it is wide. The length of the

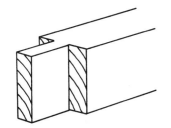

Fig. 185   Stub tenon

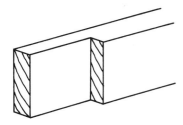

Used when the wood is thin, but not popular because of the unsightly gap which shows down one side

Fig. 186   Barefaced tenon

When the mortice has to be cut at the end, a haunch is used otherwise the joint would be a corner bridle

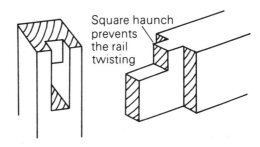

Square haunch prevents the rail twisting

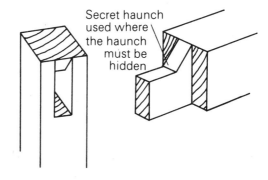

Secret haunch used where the haunch must be hidden

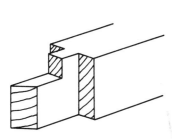

When the tenons meet at right angles as in stool construction the tenon ends must be mitred

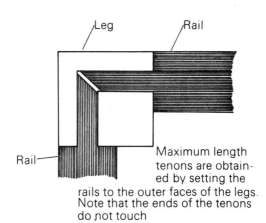

Maximum length tenons are obtained by setting the rails to the outer faces of the legs. Note that the ends of the tenons do not touch

Fig. 187   Square haunched mortice and tenon

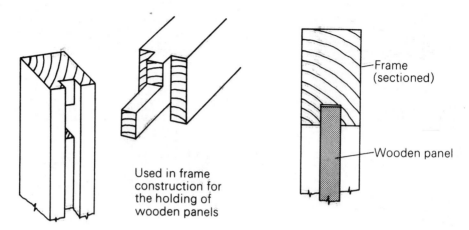

Used in frame
construction for
the holding of
wooden panels

Frame
(sectioned)

Wooden panel

Fig. 188   Grooved mortice and tenon joint

mortices and corresponding width of the tenons must be shortened by this amount and
the square haunches allowed for.

After marking out, the mortices are chopped and the tenons cut along the grain only.
The grooves are ploughed after which the tenon cheeks are sawn off.

REBATED MORTICE AND TENON JOINT, Fig. 189

When making a frame to hold a mirror or pane of glass, provision must be made for
replacement in the event of breakage. For this reason, a rebate must be made in the
frame so that removable fillets can be used to hold the glass in position. The joints are
similar to those of the grooved frame, but because of the rebate the tenon shoulders are
longer on one side and the joint is often known as the long and short shoulder mortice
and tenon.

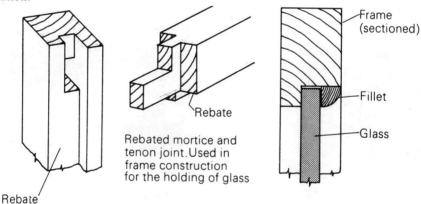

Rebate

Rebate

Rebated mortice and
tenon joint. Used in
frame construction
for the holding of glass

Frame
(sectioned)

Fillet

Glass

Fig. 189

JOINTING BOARDS

Wide boards are rare and expensive so narrow boards have to be joined edge to edge to make a wide piece of wood, say, for a table top. There are several methods by which this jointing can be done:

1. Rubbed
2. Dowelled
3. Tongue and grooved
4. Loose tongued
5. Secret slot screwed

In all cases the pieces of wood must be arranged:

(a) With the grain running in the same direction for final planing.

(b) With the heart side alternating to cancel out warping.

RUBBED JOINT, Fig. 190

The two long edges must be shot straight and true, then tested by placing one edge on top of the other before gluing. When correct, the edges are held side by side, quickly glued, and assembled. The top board is now held and rubbed firmly back and forth to expel surplus glue and bring the edges in close contact, the fingers and thumbs keeping the joint in line. After a few rubs the joint will seize and no further movement will be possible.

The work can be cramped until dry or placed against a wall using a lath to support it.

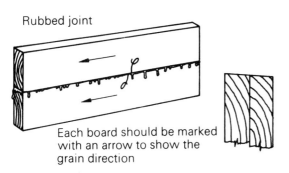

Rubbed joint

Each board should be marked with an arrow to show the grain direction

Plane the board edges together so that any error in squareness will cancel out

Fig. 190   Jointing boards

THE DOWELLED JOINT, Fig. 191

This requires care in marking out to ensure that the parts will assemble smoothly. The dowelled joint, Fig. 191, requires care in marking out to ensure that the parts will assemble smoothly. The tongue of the tongue and groove joint, Fig. 192, is weak and easily broken off because of the grain direction. A stronger form of this joint is the loose tongue which consists of a strip of plywood, Fig. 193. The secret slot screwed joint is useful where the work is required immediately, or when assembling fittings where screws must not show, Fig. 194. If necessary, the joint can be assembled dry for later

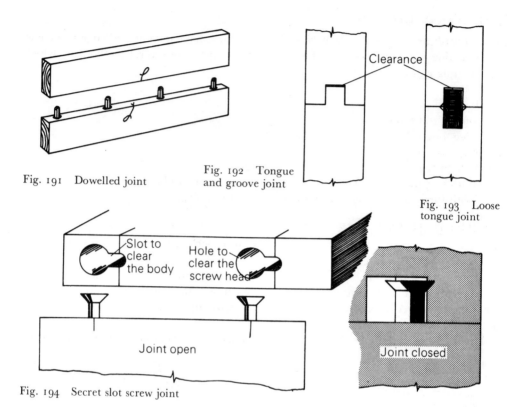

Fig. 191   Dowelled joint

Fig. 192   Tongue and groove joint

Fig. 193   Loose tongue joint

Fig. 194   Secret slot screw joint

separation. Steel screws are fixed in one piece of wood, and clearance holes for the head and body are drilled and cut in the other piece of wood. The joint is made by assembling the two parts and tapping the top part along so that the heads of the screws cut into the wooden slots.

LAPPED DOVETAILS, Fig. 195

The joint is used where the ends of the tails must not show, as on a drawer front. The wood having the pins is a little thicker than that having the tails, to allow for the lap.

The tails are marked out and chopped after shooting square the end. The pins are marked from the tails and the waste wood sawn and chiselled to the line. Because of the lap, this part is difficult. Only half the sawing can be done and the waste must be

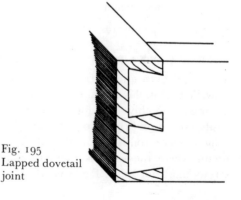

Fig. 195
Lapped dovetail joint

chopped out, carefully chiselling along and across the grain. Small bevel edge chisels are needed to clean out the acute angles of the sockets.

Making a Drawer, Fig. 196

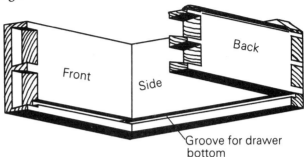

Fig. 196 Drawer with one side and bottom removed to show construction.

1. Shoot the edges and end of the FRONT to make it a push fit in the drawer opening.
2. Shoot the edges of the SIDES and the ends of the BACK to make each part a push fit in its place.
3. Plough a groove, 4 mm by 4 mm, 10 mm from the face edge, along the inside of both SIDES, but plough the groove 5 mm deep along the inside of the FRONT.
4. Pair off the SIDES, shoot the ends square and mark off the shoulder length of the dovetails.
5. Separate the SIDES, complete the marking out and cut all dovetails.
6. Mark off and chop the pins on the FRONT and BACK.
7. Round off the top edge of the BACK.
8. Clean up the inside, glue, assemble, and cramp. Test diagonals, and leave to set.
9. Fit the plywood base and fix to the underside of the BACK with screws.
   Carefully fit the drawer to its opening using a finely set smoothing plane. This requires

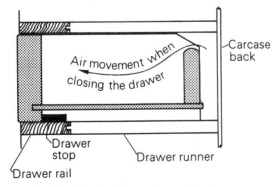

Fig. 197 Section showing drawer in position in carcase

much patience and skill because it is not always easy to see where the tight places are. This fitting is best done with the cabinet back removed so that the drawer clearance can be checked from the rear. Also, should the drawer jam while being fitted, it can be pushed free.

When fitted, finish with glasspaper and rub the sides and edges with paraffin wax to make the drawer slide easily. So that the drawer will shut in the correct position, a 50 mm strip of 6 mm plywood is fixed to the drawer rail. This is called a drawer stop, Fig. 197.

DRAWER SLIPS, Fig. 198

Instead of ploughing grooves in the drawer sides, a piece of wood about 16 mm by 10 mm can be glued to the inside of both pieces. When the glue has set, the edges are planed true and the grooves ploughed. This avoids weakening the drawer sides and is the method found in good class cabinet work. These strips of wood are called drawer slips.

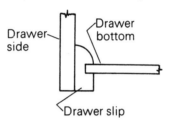

When the drawer side is too
thin to take a groove, a drawer
slip must be used

Fig. 198

Exercises

1. What are the three basic forms of construction in woodwork? Name one joint which could be used in each.

2. Why are similar lengths of wood clamped together when marking out?

3. What is a dowel? Name three important operations to obtain a well made dowelled joint.

4. A through mortice and tenon is to be made from timber 44 mm by 19 mm. Make a clear sketch and show the proportions of the various parts to ensure a strong joint.

5. Wide boards are made by edge-jointing narrow boards. Name four ways of doing this. Describe, step-by-step, how you would make one of the joints.

6. What is meant by the angle of slope of a dovetail? State what would happen if this angle were: (a) increased; (b) decreased.

7. Draw or name four ways of jointing the sides to the ends of a small box. Place a large letter 'S' against the strongest.

(WEST MIDLANDS EXAMINATIONS BOARD)

8. Describe the building of a canoe or small boat in which you have taken part, or which you have seen being built. Mention particularly methods of ensuring accuracy of shape. Use sketches where helpful.

(WEST MIDLANDS EXAMINATIONS BOARD)

9. Show, by sketches, the joints you would use for TWO of the following:
(a) the corner of a cutlery box; (b) between the leg and top rails of a stool; (c) between the shelf and side of a bookcase in hardwood.
Give reasons for your choice.

(EAST MIDLAND REGIONAL EXAMINATIONS BOARD)

10. (a) Choose two of the following, and draw a sketch to show clearly what is meant by each of the two you have chosen:
    (i)   Stopped chamfer
    (ii) Groove with loose tongue
    (iii) Stopped rebate
    (b) Give one example where each of these two could be used.

(WELSH JOINT EDUCATION COMMITTEE)

11. Why do you have a haunch on some mortice and tenon joints?

(EAST ANGLIAN REGIONAL EXAMINATIONS BOARD)

12

Construction

Constructional Processes

When constructing in solid wood, all parts must be free to shrink and expand because of changes in the moisture content of the air. Wide boards must be held in grooved frames so that they are free to move otherwise they will split, Fig. 199. These panels, as they are known, can be flat, fielded, or flush, but in all cases they must be stained and polished before assembly in their frames. If this is not done until after assembly a line of bare wood is exposed when the panel shrinks.

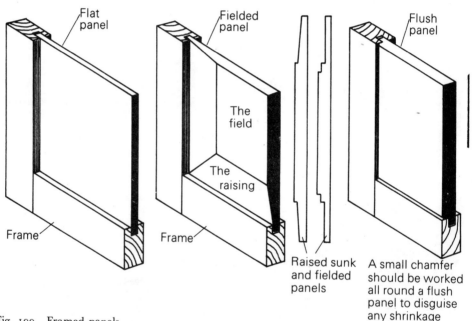

Fig. 199   Framed panels

Where a flat surface is required, such as in a drawing board, the wood is kept in shape by means of two ledges or battens screwed to the back across the grain, Fig. 200. The fixing screws are arranged in slots to allow the board to expand and contract. On large boards the tendency to warp is reduced by making several parallel shallow saw cuts

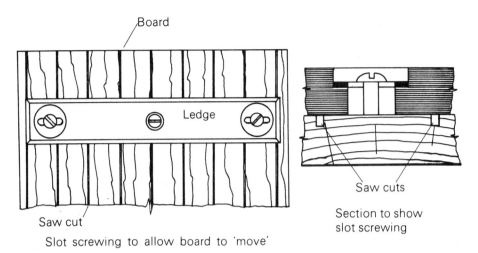

Slot screwing to allow board to 'move'

Section to show
slot screwing

Fig. 200

along the grain on the back of the board. These cut the wood fibres and break up any large twisting force into a number of smaller harmless forces.

A clamp is a strip of wood fixed across the end of a board to keep it flat. It is usual to clamp each end but unless the atmosphere is stable the board will split, Fig. 201.

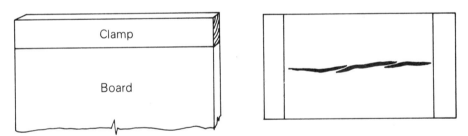

The clamp keeps the board flat but prevents movement. If the board is very wide or the work is kept in a changeable atmosphere the board will split. This often happens to clamped drawing boards

Fig. 201   Clamping

TABLE, LOCKER, AND STOOL TOPS

When made of blockboard or laminboard the top can be secured to the framework by pocket screwing. If the top overhangs the rails the pocket screwing can be angled but with a recessed top the screws must go straight through the rail centre to avoid the risk of exposing the screw points, Fig. 202. Where a solid top is fitted buttons must be used to allow for movement, Fig. 203. First, mortices are chopped at intervals in all rails, or a groove can be ploughed for quickness before assembly.

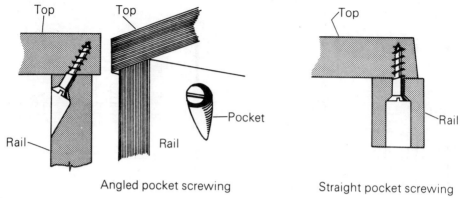

Angled pocket screwing   Straight pocket screwing

Fig. 202

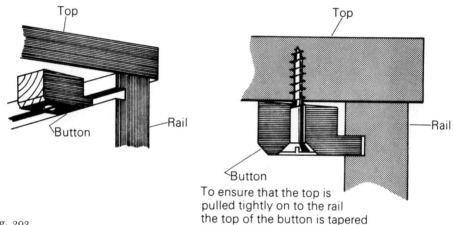

To ensure that the top is
pulled tightly on to the rail
the top of the button is tapered

Fig. 203

GLUE BLOCKS, Fig. 204

These are blocks of wood fitted and glued to inside corners to strengthen the work. A piece of squared wood is sawn diagonally along its length and planed smooth. The corner should be planed off to ensure that the faces of the glue block bear against the work. Each block is lightly glued, pressed into position and moved back and forth until it siezes in place. The inside corners of large frames, boxes, and butt joints may have to be reinforced with glue blocks.

DOORS

Flush doors can be made by using blockboard and lipping the edges. A lighter door can be made by constructing a frame and facing both sides with plywood or hardboard, Fig. 205.

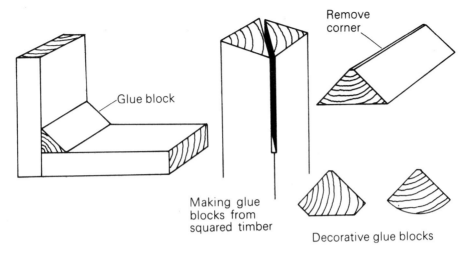

Remove corner

Glue block

Making glue blocks from squared timber

Decorative glue blocks

Fig. 204

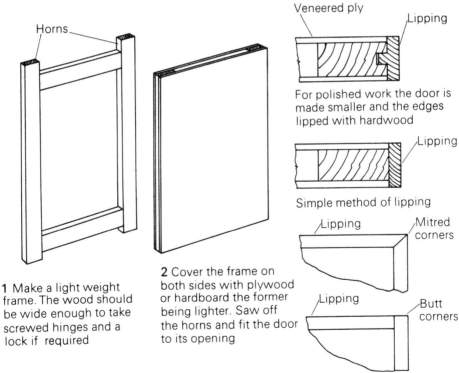

Horns

Veneered ply

Lipping

For polished work the door is made smaller and the edges lipped with hardwood

Lipping

Simple method of lipping

Lipping

Mitred corners

Lipping

Butt corners

1 Make a light weight frame. The wood should be wide enough to take screwed hinges and a lock if required

2 Cover the frame on both sides with plywood or hardboard the former being lighter. Saw off the horns and fit the door to its opening

Fig. 205   Built-up doors

PLASTIC LAMINATES

Read the maker's instructions and be sure you understand what you have to do. Two important things are:

1. Saw from the patterned side to avoid breaking this surface, and
2. Protect the finished edges by chamfering them.

Where the edges of a board are to be covered as well as the top, apply the plastic to the edges first, then the top last. A smooth file can be used for the final trimming of the plastic edges, but a scraper plane is ideal for quickly removing waste plastic from the edges.

RECESSING AND OVERHANGING, Fig. 206

Where possible, avoid assembling two parts with their surfaces in line. Sooner or later there will be some movement of the wood and the work will appear to have been badly fitted. This is avoided by fitting one part about 3 mm in front of or behind the other to make a 'break'. Not only does this make the parts easier to assemble but it looks better, resulting in lights and shadows having a pleasing effect. Drawers should be made to stand in slightly from their surrounding framework though there may be occasions

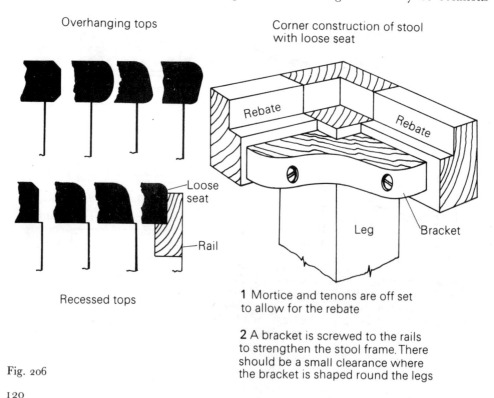

Overhanging tops

Corner construction of stool
with loose seat

Rebate

Rebate

Loose
seat

Rail

Recessed tops

Leg

Bracket

1 Mortice and tenons are off set
to allow for the rebate

2 A bracket is screwed to the rails
to strengthen the stool frame. There
should be a small clearance where
the bracket is shaped round the legs

Fig. 206

120

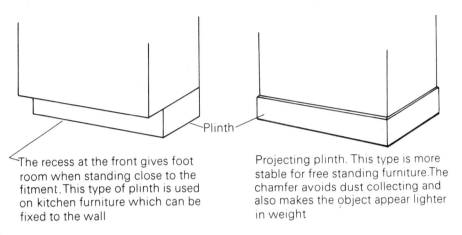

The recess at the front gives foot room when standing close to the fitment. This type of plinth is used on kitchen furniture which can be fixed to the wall

Projecting plinth. This type is more stable for free standing furniture.The chamfer avoids dust collecting and also makes the object appear lighter in weight

Fig. 207

when they would look better projecting. Stool tops can be recessed slightly or overhang quite a lot depending on their use. Lockers and bookcases may stand on frames called plinths, Fig. 207. For balance, these should project but may look too heavy. If they are made to recede, care must be taken to check the stability of the finished work.

FITTING A GLASS PANE, Fig. 208

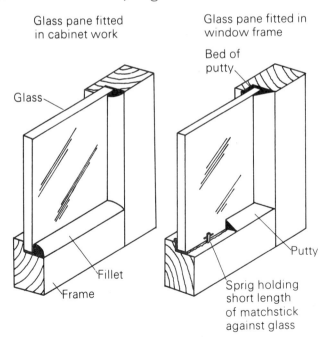

Glass pane fitted in cabinet work

Glass pane fitted in window frame

Bed of putty

Glass

Fillet

Frame

Putty

Sprig holding short length of matchstick against glass

Fig. 208

The glass should be cut 1.5 mm shorter in length and width to make it an easy fit in the frame. To hold the glass in position, fillets are made by mitring and fitting lengths of moulding. Drill holes for the panel pins and tap each fillet in place, taking care not to let the fillet press against the glass. Continue mitring and fitting each fillet until all four have been nailed in position. If preferred, screws **can** be used for fixing.

Where the joint must be waterproof, as in a window pane, putty is used. This is a mixture of linseed oil and whiting and is stored in an airtight container or a tin of water to keep it soft. The rebate is first painted with a priming coat and then an undercoat. This is essential to stop the linseed oil soaking into the bare wood and leaving a dry powder. Press a little soft putty all round the rebate and gently squeeze the pane in place so that it rests on a bed of putty. Secure the glass in position with a few brads by sliding the hammer on the pane to tap the brads in the rebate. A short length of match-stick between the glass and the brad acts as a cushion. Finally, putty all round the rebate and trim off the surplus from both sides using a knife. After leaving for a few days to dry, the frame can be painted.

FITTING A MIRROR FRAME, Fig. 209

The rebate should be painted with a dull black paint as used in cameras to prevent reflection through the mirror edge. The frame is laid flat on the bench and the mirror placed centrally in position. On no account must the back of the mirror be touched in case the surface is scratched. Wedged fillets, about 50 mm long, are carefully placed in position and fixed with panel pins. Alternatively, the fillets can be glued in place like glue blocks and the projecting edges afterwards planed smooth. A thin piece of plywood is screwed to the back of the frame to complete the work.

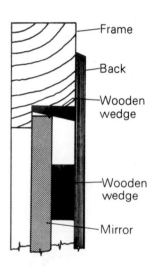

Mirror fitted in frame

Frame

Back

Wooden wedge

Wooden wedge

Mirror

The tapered wedges support the mirror at its edges

Fig. 209

CONSTRUCTION USING DRAWERS, Fig. 210

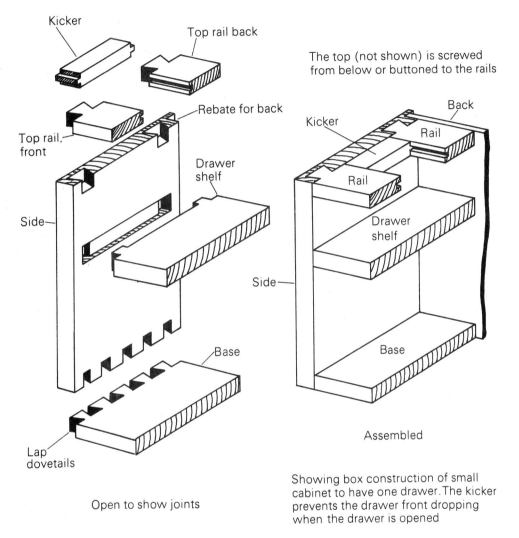

Kicker

Top rail back

The top (not shown) is screwed
from below or buttoned to the rails

Top rail, front

Rebate for back

Kicker

Back

Rail

Drawer shelf

Side

Rail

Drawer shelf

Side

Base

Base

Lap dovetails

Open to show joints

Assembled

Showing box construction of small
cabinet to have one drawer. The kicker
prevents the drawer front dropping
when the drawer is opened

Fig. 210

For small work, solid ends and shelves are quite suitable. On larger work, Fig. 211, framing is used both for lightness in weight and economy of timber. Once, a panel called a dust board was fitted in the groove running round the drawer rail, runners, and back rail, but this is seldom seen today for reasons of economy.

123

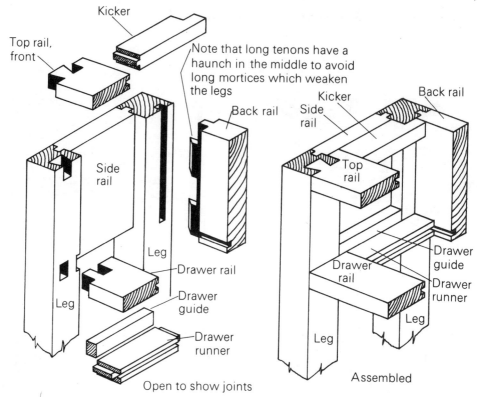

Kicker

Top rail, front

Note that long tenons have a haunch in the middle to avoid long mortices which weaken the legs

Back rail

Side rail

Kicker

Side rail

Back rail

Top rail

Leg

Drawer rail

Leg

Drawer guide

Leg

Drawer runner

Drawer guide

Drawer rail

Drawer guide

Drawer runner

Leg

Open to show joints

Leg

Assembled

Fig. 211 Showing stool construction of small table to have one drawer

BUTT HINGES, Fig. 212

These are commonly called 'butts' and are used for the hingeing of doors. They are made of cast iron, steel, pressed brass, and solid brass, this last type being very strong and popular for good class work because the knuckle cannot open out under heavy pressure. For most work two hinges are sufficient, but for heavy doors three must be used.

To fit a pair of butt hinges. First of all fit the door to its opening. If the woodwork is to be painted there should be a full 2 mm clearance all round to allow for the thickness of the paint, but if the wood is to be polished, 0.5 mm clearance is ample.

For work to be painted, mark off the position of the hinges on the door, then mark off the hinge length from the hinge, Fig. 213. Set a marking gauge from the leaf edge to the knuckle centre, Fig. 214, and gauge the leaf-width on the door stile. Set a different marking gauge to the leaf thickness, Fig. 215, and gauge the wood, Fig. 216. By using two marking gauges they can each be set once and used later for the surround or carcase. Chisel out the waste wood exactly to the line, place one leaf of each hinge in position and

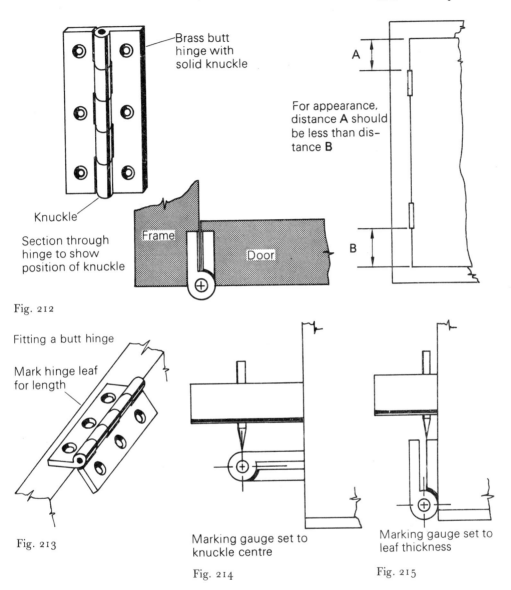

Brass butt hinge with solid knuckle

Knuckle

Section through hinge to show position of knuckle

For appearance, distance **A** should be less than distance **B**

Fig. 212

Fitting a butt hinge

Mark hinge leaf for length

Fig. 213

Marking gauge set to knuckle centre

Fig. 214

Marking gauge set to leaf thickness

Fig. 215

hold with one screw. Now position the door with equal clearance at top and bottom and mark off the hinge positions on the carcase. Square across all four lines, and gauge to width and thickness. Chop out the waste, place each leaf in position, and hold with one screw. Test by opening and closing the door several times. In particular, test that the door will stay closed. If it springs open a little, check that the screws fit right in their countersunk holes. If these are properly fitted then the door is 'hinge bound', which

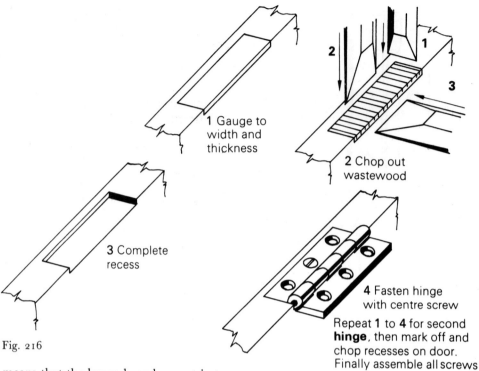

1 Gauge to width and thickness

2 Chop out wastewood

3 Complete recess

4 Fasten hinge with centre screw

Repeat **1** to **4** for second **hinge**, then mark off and chop recesses on door. Finally assemble all screws

Fig. 216

means that the leaves have been set in too deeply and must be packed out with veneer. When the door opens and closes correctly affix all the screws.

When fitting hinges in first class cabinet work it is usual to set the marking gauge to the knuckle centre of the hinge, but a moment's thought will show that this will cause hinge binding. Unless the parts are dead flat and perfectly straight, the door will not close because such a gauge setting does not allow for any clearance between the hanging stile and the carcase. For a good fit, therefore, allow half the door clearance when setting the marking gauge, Fig. 217. Except for this one setting the method of fitting the hinges is exactly as for the painted work. A door stop, consisting of a strip of wood, should

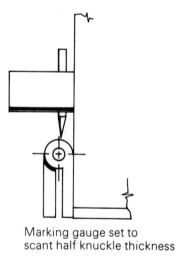

Marking gauge set to scant half knuckle thickness

Fig. 217

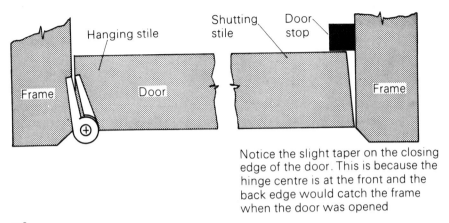

Notice the slight taper on the closing edge of the door. This is because the hinge centre is at the front and the back edge would catch the frame when the door was opened

Fig. 218

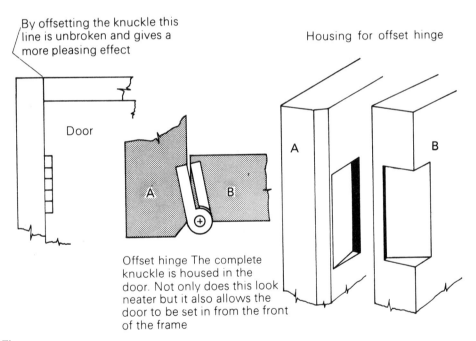

By offsetting the knuckle this line is unbroken and gives a more pleasing effect

Housing for offset hinge

Door

Offset hinge The complete knuckle is housed in the door. Not only does this look neater but it also allows the door to be set in from the front of the frame

Fig. 219

be screwed inside the cabinet against which the door can close, Fig. 218.

To avoid breaking the vertical line of the door edge it is usual to set the knuckle end of the hinge in the door but with the leaves slanting outwards and with one leaf fitted in the carcase so that the weight of the door is not hanging on the screws, Fig. 219.

BACK-FLAP HINGES, Fig. 220

These have wider leaves and are screwed to the faces of work such as the drop leaf of a table.

T-HINGES

These hinges, or cross garnet hinges, are made in three strengths: light, medium, and strong, and may be had with either a bright or japanned black finish, Fig. 221.

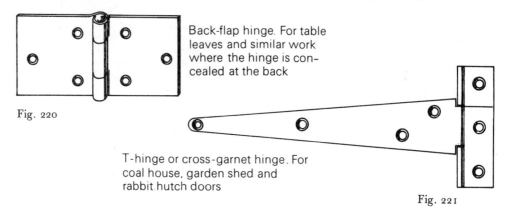

Back-flap hinge. For table leaves and similar work where the hinge is concealed at the back

Fig. 220

T-hinge or cross-garnet hinge. For coal house, garden shed and rabbit hutch doors

Fig. 221

STRAIGHT CUPBOARD LOCK, Fig. 222

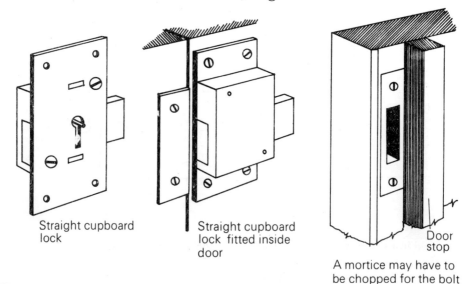

Straight cupboard lock

Straight cupboard lock fitted inside door

Door stop

A mortice may have to be chopped for the bolt to enter

Fig. 222

A simple lock, obtainable in steel and brass and having from one to four levers. The more levers a lock has the more difficult it is to open it with a different key. In this type, the bolt is made to open both sides so that the lock can be fitted to right- and left-handed doors. When a door opens towards you it is right-handed if the hinges are on the right, and left-handed if hinged on the left.

Straight cupboard locks are suitable where the carcase is the same thickness as the door or where two doors meet. In both cases, the door stop would have to be fitted to the top and bottom of the carcase.

Fitting a straight cupboard lock, Fig. 223. Square a pencil line across the middle of the shutting stile of the door. Set the marking gauge to half the width of the lock plus 2 mm for clearance. Cut the pencil line with this gauge setting and drill the keyhole with waste wood clamped to the rear of the door to prevent splintering. Complete the slot with a mortice chisel, then hammer in a brass escutcheon. An escutcheon plate can be fitted instead if desired, but something should be done to protect the wood from fraying. Insert the key and place the lock in position operating the key to check that there are no obstructions. Screw the lock to the door to complete the job.

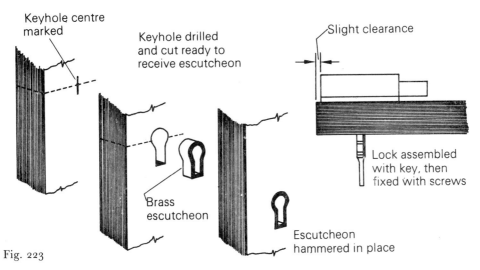

Keyhole centre marked

Keyhole drilled and cut ready to receive escutcheon

Slight clearance

Brass escutcheon

Escutcheon hammered in place

Lock assembled with key, then fixed with screws

Fig. 223

CUT CUPBOARD LOCK, Fig. 224

This is made to sink into the side of a door so that it operates from the door edge. After squaring a pencil line across the middle of the shutting stile, set the marking gauge from the edge of the lock to the pin centre. Mark this distance on the pencil line and drill and cut the keyhole to suit. Place the key in the door, position the lock and mark out the lock housing. Chop out the waste, then position the lock and key again to mark out the back plate. Chop out this waste, screw the lock in place, and test with the key. Smear the

Cut cupboard lock. Also known as a till lock because the two way keyhole enables it to be used on drawers

Cut the keyhole. Mark out and chop the recess for the lock, then mark out and chop the recess for the lock plate

Fig. 224

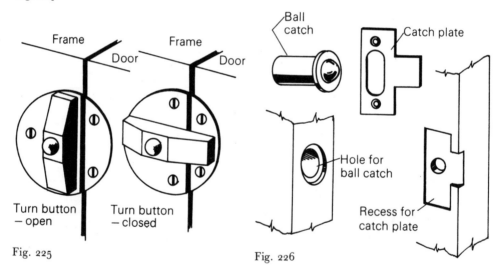

Fig. 225

Fig. 226

end of the bolt with used oil from the oilstone, close the door and turn the key to mark the carcase for the bolt slot. This can be chopped out with a mortice chisel and looks better if protected with a brass plate.

For the closing of painted doors, cupboard buttons are normally used, Fig. 225, but for polished work, ball catches are to be preferred for their neater appearance, Fig. 226. Magnetic door catches are strong, silent, and easy to fit. There are several strengths for different sized doors.

Exercises

1. Where would you use glue blocks? How would you fit them?

2. Where would you find:
   (a) a drawer rail, (b) drawer runner, (c) drawer guide, (d) a kicker?

3. Allowance for the expansion and contraction of timber should be a major consideration in the design of any article made from solid timber. Explain, with the aid of sketches, three different methods of overcoming this problem.
   (MIDDLESEX REGIONAL EXAMINING BOARD)

4. Name two articles that you could make using a framed construction.
   (SOUTHERN REGIONAL EXAMINATIONS BOARD)

5. Sketch: (a) a butt hinge, (b) a back-flap hinge.
   (SOUTHERN REGIONAL EXAMINATIONS BOARD)

6. Say what you know about shrinkage in timber, and show by sketches and notes a method used for permitting movement in ONE of the following constructions:
   (a) making a door with a solid panel;
   (b) fixing a solid table top to an underframing.
   (EAST MIDLAND REGIONAL EXAMINATIONS BOARD)

7. What are the reasons for chamfering the edge of a stool or table top?
   (WEST MIDLANDS EXAMINATIONS BOARD)

8. The door of a small cabinet is to be hung by means of a pair of 38 mm brass butt hinges.
   (a) Show, by means of sketches and notes, how the waste on the door is marked and cut out to receive one of the hinges.
   (b) Give TWO probable causes why a hinged door refuses to stay completely closed.
   (WELSH JOINT EDUCATION COMMITTEE)

13

Wood Finishes

Wood must be finished in some way to protect it and keep it clean, as well as to improve its appearance. In general, softwoods are painted, and hardwoods are polished or varnished to enrich the natural beauty of the wood. Sometimes, the wood is stained before polishing to improve its colour and show more clearly the figure and grain.

Wood stopping is a clay-like material moistened with water to form a paste, and used for filling nail holes and cracks. The stopping is pressed in place with a knife blade and when hard, rubbed smooth with glass paper. If, for some reason, putty has to be used instead, it must be applied after the undercoat.

Knotting is similar to french polish and is used to seal knots. If this is not done, the resin in the knot will discolour and spoil the paint at some later date.

PAINT

Bare wood requires a primer, one or two undercoats and a finishing or top coat of paint. Primer must be applied to seal the bare wood and prevent the oil in the undercoat soaking in. For outdoor work, a lead-based primer is advisable. As this is very poisonous great care must be taken during painting, rubbing down must be done with water and 'wet or dry' abrasive paper to prevent dust, and the hands well washed afterwards. For indoor work, especially, toys, avoid all paints having a lead base. Aluminium wood primer is a safe and easily applied paint.

The undercoat provides a smooth surface of good even colour for the top coat. Both the primer and undercoat are difficult to apply because there is little oil in the paint. This work requires care to avoid brush marks which would spoil the finished appearance. The top coat is an oil paint consisting mainly of colouring pigment mixed with refined linseed oil and a little white spirit or thinners. Enamel paint is oil paint to which gums and resins have been added.

Stir the paint from the bottom of the can using a clean stick and thoroughly mix the pigment with the oil. When finished painting, tap the lid firmly in place and invert the can momentarily. This seals the contents and prevents a skin forming during long storage periods.

When painting with a brush, use only the end of the bristles and spread the paint over the work in vertical and horizontal strokes, finishing off vertically. Remember that two thin coats are better than one thick coat.

After use, clean the brushes by wiping them on a piece of scrap wood to remove as much paint as possible. Rinse the bristles in clean white spirit, then wash in soap and hot water. Finally, rinse in warm water and place flat on a shelf to dry. Never leave brushes standing in a jar for long periods. This causes the bristles to bend out of shape.

All finishing should be done in a clean, dry, warm room, quite free from dust.

Resinous woods, such as pitch pine, do not take paint very well and should be avoided in the making of jobs to be painted. Where this is unavoidable, the wood should be given one or two coats of knotting (thinned with methylated spirits) before painting.

METHOD OF PAINTING

1. Rub the surface across the grain with No. 1 glass paper. Dust clean.
2. Seal any knots with a coat of knotting.
   Drying time: about 4 hours.
3. Apply a coat of undercoat paint.
   Drying time: about 12 hours.
4. Fill any holes and cracks with stopping. When hard, rub smooth with glass paper and dust clean.
5. Apply a top coat of oil paint or enamel.
   Drying time: at least 24 hours.

For an excellent finish, the top coat is rubbed down when hard, using a wet cloth and pumice powder. This provides a smooth dull surface to which a second top coat can be applied.

STAINS

There are three types of stains:
1. Water
2. Spirit
3. Oil

Water stains are cheap and are made by dissolving coloured powders and crystals in boiling water. Vandyke crystals gives a very popular brown stain, especially suitable for use on light coloured woods such as oak. A strong solution should be made and the liquid diluted to give the required shade. End grain is sized before staining to prevent excess stain being absorbed and making this part much darker than the rest of the wood. Another method is to dilute the stain.

Unfortunately, water stain raises the grain so the wood should be wiped over with warm water and the raised grain rubbed smooth before staining. The stain is applied with a flat brush then rubbed well in with a cloth and left to dry before any further work is done.

Spirit stains consist of coloured powders dissolved in methylated spirits. It is difficult to get an even colour with a spirit stain because it dries very quickly. A brush is used and the work covered as rapidly as possible to prevent the 'live' or wet edge drying out. If this happens the colour will show as streaks. This type of stain is not recommended for ordinary use.

133

Oil stains are bought ready for use and are easy to apply. They do not raise the grain and being slow drying produce an evenly coloured surface. The stain is applied with a brush and left for several hours to dry, then the wood is rubbed with a clean rag to remove any oil remaining on the surface. Proprietary oil stains are available in a wide range of colours and many are referred to as dyes because, it is claimed, they have deeper penetrating powers than a stain.

Filler is a paste used for filling in the grain to make the surface smooth. This is a quicker and cheaper method than applying many coats of varnish and rubbing down each coat. Fine-textured woods do not require a filler nor do woods which are to be waxed. Coarse-grained woods, such as oak, should not be filled because this spoils the appearance of the wood. Whiting or dental plaster (a fine plaster of paris) can be used to fill the grain, but proprietary brands of wood filler are available in paste form in different colours and ready for use. After staining, the filler is rubbed firmly into the grain with a cloth using a circular motion. A piece of clean cloth is then used to wipe off the surplus filler by rubbing across the grain. When dry, the surface is lightly rubbed smooth and dusted.

Wax polish is made by shredding beeswax into a tin and heating it in a pan of water to melt it. Pure turpentine is added to form a soft paste (**warning:** DO NOT add the turpentine near a flame). A high polish is obtained by spreading a thin film of wax polish over the wood using a rag or brush and leaving it for several hours to let the turpentine evaporate. The surface is then vigorously rubbed with a brush and finished with a duster. This must be repeated several times to produce a pleasant satin shine which is improved if the wood is first given one or two coats of french polish.

French polish was once a popular method of finishing hardwood. Much skill was necessary, the process took several days and resulted in a thin, transparent gloss. Unfortunately, its use is limited because it does not resist heat and water. French polish is made by dissolving shellac in methylated spirits. Shellac is obtained from a crust which forms on the body of insects found on certain trees mainly in India. The polish dries very quickly and is used to seal oil stain so that the stain will not be affected by the turpentine if wax polished.

Hardwood Finishes

There are many proprietary brands of modern wood finishes which are simple and easy to use, and give excellent results. In many cases a hard, tough surface which resists heat and water can be obtained. Be careful not to use different kinds of stain and polish; stick to one brand throughout.

The following finishes are suggested because they are simple and effective, but others can be worked out from the different materials available.

Wax finish

1. Stain, if required.
2. Fill the grain, if necessary. When dry, lightly rub down with flour paper. Dust clean.

3. Apply a coat of french polish with a brush. When dry, rub down with flour paper. Dust clean.
4. Apply a second coat of french polish. When dry, rub down with flour paper. Dust clean.
5. Apply a thin film of wax polish to the wood using a brush or clean rag. Leave for several hours because no shine is possible until the turpentine has evaporated.
6. Rub hard with a stiff brush and finish with a cloth.
7. Repeat 5 and 6, several times for a good finish.

Varnish finish, using a polyurethane varnish
1. Stain, if required. Use a polyurethane stain.
2. Fill the grain, if necessary. Use a polyurethane filler. When dry, lightly rub down with flour paper. Dust clean.
3. Apply a coat of polyurethane varnish with a brush. Drying and hardening time: about 6 hours.
4. Rub down with oo steel wool. Dust clean.
5. Apply a second coat of polyurethane varnish. Drying and hardening time: about 6 hours.

This finish is heat and water resistant. On fine-textured woods the first coat can act as a filler, in which case three coats of varnish may be necessary.

Oil finish
1. Stain, if required.
2. Fill the grain, if necessary. Lightly rub down with flour paper. Dust clean.
3. Apply a coat of teak oil, rubbing it well in the wood with a rag. Wipe off the surplus oil.
   Drying time: about 8 hours.
4. Apply a coat of teak oil daily for several days until a mellow shine is obtained.

Note: Teak oil is made from tung oil obtained from the seeds of trees found in China. Teak oil is quick drying and does not darken the wood as does linseed oil, which it has now replaced for this type of finish.

Plastic Coat

This new type of finish is obtained by the chemical hardening of synthetic resins. A small kit is purchased which contains the plastic coating, the hardener, thinners for cleaning the brushes, and burnishing material which may be in a powder or liquid form. The required amount of plastic hardener is measured into a glass jar and the hardener added. The work proceeds as follows:
1. Stain if required, using proprietary stains.
2. Fill the grain if necessary, using proprietary filler for this type of finish.
3. Apply a coat of plastic coating with a brush.
   Drying time: 2 hours in a warm room.
4. Lightly rub down with flour paper. Dust clean.

5. Apply the second coat of plastic coating.
   Drying and hardening time: 8 hours.
6. Lightly rub down with flour paper. Dust clean.
   This will have produced a matt surface. To obtain a bright gloss surface use the burnishing paste as follows:
7. Rub the burnishing paste along the work in straight lines, using a damp cloth. Begin with hard pressure and gradually reduce to light pressure.
8. Polish with a duster.

Note: Plastic coating is hard, tough, and resistant to heat and water. Once dry, it cannot be dissolved so the brushes must be cleaned each time after use in the special thinners provided in the kit.

Outdoor Work

To preserve timber used outdoors, such as fences, the wood must be poisoned to prevent attack by fungi and insects. The cheapest way of doing this is to soak the wood in a large drum of hot creosote if possible otherwise it must be given one or two coats with a brush.

Finishes for Turned Work

1. Apply one coat of wood sealer, polyurethane varnish or french polish. When hard rub down with oo steel wool. Dust clean.
2. Apply a lump of carnauba wax to the revolving wood so as to leave a thin film of wax.
3. Polish with a pad of cloth.

Note: Carnauba wax is harder than beeswax and is of vegetable origin.

Other finishes can also be obtained including plastic coating. Rubbing down is done with a steel wool pad while the work is revolving.

Exercises

1. Wood very often has a finish applied to it. Why is this necessary? What finishes would be suitable for:
   (i)   a whitewood bathroom cabinet;
   (ii) the part of a gatepost which is sunk into the ground;
   (iii) an oak bookcase;
   (iv) a finely figured table top?
   Give reasons for your choice in each case.

(MIDDLESEX REGIONAL EXAMINING BOARD)

2. Give brief 'step by step' outline information (numbered 1, 2, 3, etc.) to provide protective finishes for the following newly constructed jobs:
   (in each case let the heading for step No. 1 be 'glasspapering')

(a) a greenhouse, constructed in European redwood;
(b) a solid oak table, requring a natural finish;
(c) a mahogany table, requiring a high gloss finish.

(SOUTH-EAST REGIONAL EXAMINATIONS BOARD)

3. Mention three different types of 'surface finish' and the woods for which they would be most suitable. Describe in detail how you obtained a good surface finish on a piece of work.

(EAST MIDLAND REGIONAL EXAMINATIONS BOARD)

4. Give detailed reasons for the uses of the following 'finishes' to woodwork, and give an example of when you would use each one:
(a) french polish or synthetic polish
(b) linseed oil or teak oil
(c) creosote

(SOUTHERN REGIONAL EXAMINATIONS BOARD)

5. Explain the difference between stopping and filling.

14
Design

Design means everything which must be considered for the production of a piece of work, and includes:
1. The function or purpose of the piece of work
2. Size
3. Shape
4. Material
5. Joints
6. Decoration
7. Glue
8. Fittings
9. Colour
10. Finish

FUNCTION

The piece of work must fulfil its function. A chair must be strong and comfortable to sit on, and a standard lamp should be quite stable and cast its light where required.

SIZE

Begin with the size. If designing a pencil box, experiment with thin card to find the size and shape of the box that will hold the pencils. Decide on the thickness of wood, and the outside measurements can then be found.

The width of a room door-space must be known before deciding the width of a tea trolley, after which the other sizes can be fixed. In every case, it is advisable to check the main sizes at least twice before proceeding.

SHAPE

From the beginning of man's existence he has had an urge to shape things to give him pleasure. It is not enough to assemble a few pieces of wood to make something. No matter how well it serves its purpose it must be pleasing to look at. Man's nature demands this.

When we look at something our eye explores the outline of the shape in an effort to understand it. If this shape is uninteresting, like the square and the circle, the eye quickly tires and we say we dislike it. If, however, the shape is elliptical, rectangular, or has an odd number of sides we like it, and if the proportions are good it will always give

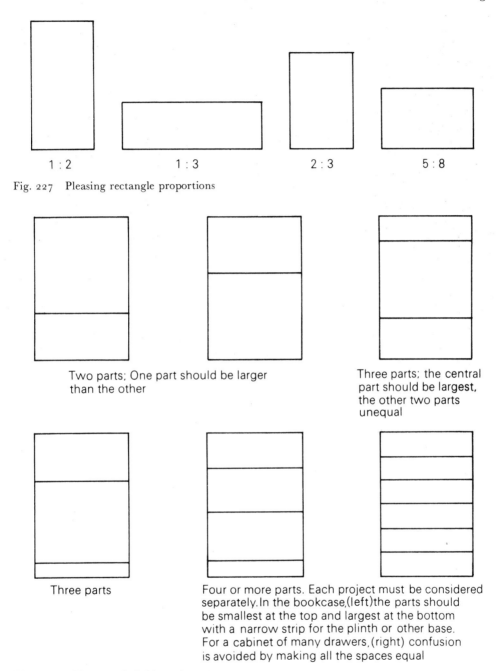

Fig. 227   Pleasing rectangle proportions

1 : 2   1 : 3   2 : 3   5 : 8

Two parts; One part should be larger
than the other

Three parts; the central
part should be largest,
the other two parts
unequal

Three parts

Four or more parts. Each project must be considered
separately. In the bookcase, (left) the parts should
be smallest at the top and largest at the bottom
with a narrow strip for the plinth or other base.
For a cabinet of many drawers, (right) confusion
is avoided by making all the spaces equal

Fig. 228a   Horizontal division of a unit

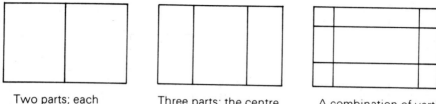

Two parts; each
should be equal

Three parts; the centre
part should be the largest
to avoid looking squashed,
and the other two parts
should be equal

A combination of vertical
and horizontal divisions.
By moving the lines a variety
of designs can be made

Fig. 228b   Vertical
divisions of a unit

pleasure. This is because the eye never tires of exploring an outline which it cannot
readily understand. This does not mean that the shape should be complicated for this
would only confuse and irritate.

Rectangles, with sides in some definite proportion such as 1:2, 1:3, or 2:3, are much
more interesting than the plain square, Fig. 227. The Greeks enjoyed a rectangle having
sides in the proportion of 5:8, which they called the 'golden oblong'. When dividing
these rectangles to give shelf, drawer, and cupboard space, care must be taken to make
the divisions interesting, Fig. 228.

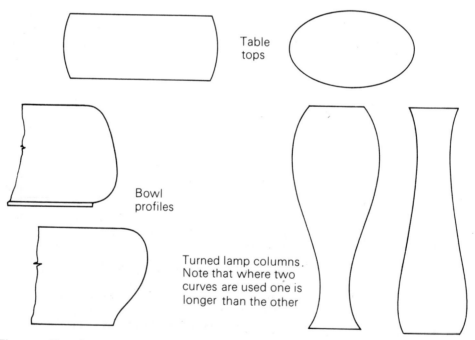

Table
tops

Bowl
profiles

Turned lamp columns.
Note that where two
curves are used one is
longer than the other

Fig. 229   Use of curves to give a pleasing shape

140

Most of us find the scenery of hills and valleys more attractive than flat plains, and motorists usually have difficulty in keeping awake on long stretches of straight roads because they find it monotonous. In woodwork, shapes can be made much more interesting by using slight curves in suitable places, Fig. 229.

MATERIAL

For outdoor work, durable timber should be used, and timber prices must be carefully weighed against the type of job and how long it has to last. For indoor work, hardwood is chosen for appearance and strength though softwood, being cheaper, would be used for structural work and fitments which are to be painted. Large areas such as doors, table tops, and the backs of furniture may require one of the built-up boards, such as plywood and blockboard, either plain or veneered with wood or a decorative laminate.

It is an important stage in the production of a piece of hardwood furniture to select each piece of timber with regard to its grain, figure, and general appearance. This requires a large stock of wood to allow selection and rejection, and timber merchants usually charge more for selected timber because of the extra time and effort required.

JOINTS

Joints should be as simple as possible and arranged to give strength and support.

Although modern glues are so good that joints appear to be unnecessary, the standard of accuracy required is extremely high when cutting parts to size. Assembly is also difficult because the parts slip about too easily. For bench workers, best results are obtained by cutting joints with shoulders against which the parts will close when assembled.

GLUE

The type of glue depends on whether the work is for internal use or not. For indoor use, most glues would be suitable for the majority of jobs, but for external work — such as boats and beehives — waterproof glue is essential. Once again, the cost should be considered where there is a choice of glue.

DECORATION, Fig. 230

Decoration must serve some purpose and should be kept to a minimum. The simplest form of decoration is the chamfer which is used to give an appearance of lightness to the work, as well as creating a light and shadow effect. The chamfer may run the whole length of the edge or be stopped. Wood of a contrasting colour can be inlaid or let into the surface, either as a pattern or in the form of a line. Veneer can also be used to bring colour and pattern to a small plain surface.

FITTINGS

These include such items as hinges, handles, hooks, locks, and ball catches, as well as nails, panel pins, and screws.

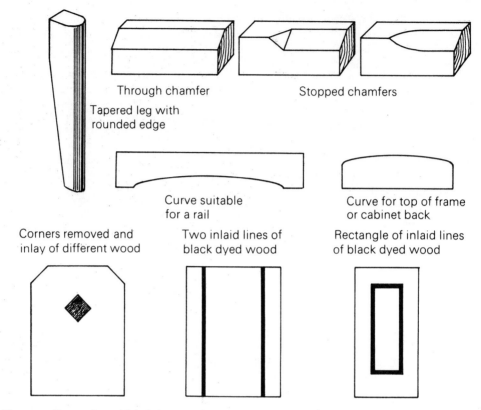

Through chamfer   Stopped chamfers

Tapered leg with
rounded edge

Curve suitable
for a rail

Curve for top of frame
or cabinet back

Corners removed and
inlay of different wood

Two inlaid lines of
black dyed wood

Rectangle of inlaid lines
of black dyed wood

Fig. 230   Decoration which lightens the appearance of the work and creates interest

COLOUR

Colour is very important to us—it can please or depress. Imagine living in a room painted black. Green is a restful colour, red appears warm, while blue has a cold effect.

Few timbers are seen at their best unless stained, oak is too pale, while the mahoganies have a 'muddy' brown colour. For this reason it is usual to stain timber which has to be polished. If in doubt, experiment on scrap wood, remembering that the purpose of staining is to improve the appearance of the timber. Oak is usually toned down to a honey colour or a warm light brown, while mahogany is stained a golden brown or a rich dark red.

FINISH

It is usual to paint softwoods, but hardwoods chosen for their beauty must have a transparent finish. Coarse-grained timbers, such as oak, should be waxed, but the fine-grained mahoganies and walnuts may be waxed or given two coats of varnish or some other modern finish.

A Design Problem and one Solution

A woodworker in a small workshop kept his nails in tin boxes and glass jars which were sometimes knocked over or mislaid causing much annoyance and waste of time. The solution to this problem was a better method of storing nails. Because of this need the woodworker decided to make a single box with separate compartments and this posed the following questions: How big would the box have to be? How many compartments should it have? What sizes ought they to be? What joints should be used? Is the box to be a fixture or portable? What is the best wood to use? What would be the most suitable finish?

The first step was to list the nail sizes, and this depended on the thickness of timber generally used in the workshops. It was finally decided on a range of nails from 13 mm to 38 mm long, and thus the compartments were fixed at 100 mm long to give ample room for the long nails. The widths of the compartments were varied to allow for the increase in nail size, but as this increase in width was in sequence from left to right and not haphazard, it was not confusing.

Hardwood was chosen being considered necessary for good wearing qualities. Dovetail joints were designed for the corners because of their strength and ease of positive assembly, and stopped housing joints for the partitions. Three-millimetre beech-faced plywood was considered suitable for the base.

A number of sketches were made, and from the final one an overall size of 350 mm long by 120 mm wide, using 10 mm thick timber was found to be functional. The rectangular shape was improved by making it 360 mm long to give it a proportion of 3:1, the slight increase being useful in the compartments, Fig. 231. A cardboard model was made to test the quantity of nails which could be held together with ease of removal, and a depth of 35 mm was found satisfactory. It was then discovered that small nails were difficult to grip at the bottom of the compartment and got 'lost' in the corners.

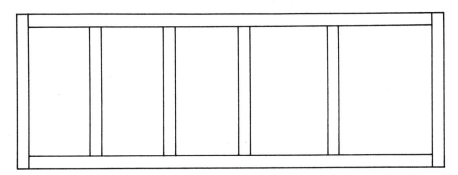

Fig. 231   Plan of the nail box finally accepted after many experiments

After some thought, three solutions presented themselves:
1. Fix a piece of plywood, curved from front to back, in each compartment.

2. Cut and shape a block of wood to fit in each compartment.
3. Fix glue blocks at each end of the compartments.

After considering each, the last solution was decided on and the box was made, assembled with resin glue and finished with two thin coats of good varnish, Fig. 232. Later a hinged lid was designed and fitted to protect the contents of the box from dust and shavings, Fig. 233.

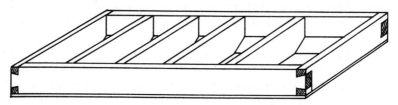

Fig. 232   The nail box showing V-blocks at ends to make the withdrawal of nails easier

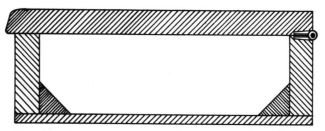

Fig. 233   Section through nail box after hinged lid had been added to keep shavings and dust out of the box

At some later date, the woodworker noticed the ease with which coins could be slid out of the hollowed bowls in cash tills. It appeared that if large coins could be slipped out of a bowl with ease then bowls could be the ideal shape for the storage and dispensing of small nails which are difficult to pick up. Each bowl would have to be turned from a square block of wood and the blocks afterwards joined together, Fig. 234. Hardwood is too expensive, so softwood must be used but a plastic coat will give a hard protective coat to the wood.

Can you take over the problems of design from here? Can you design a nail box

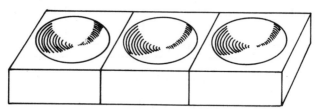

Fig. 234   Showing proposed bowl type nail box

consisting of a number of bowls? How would you join them together? What would be the best bowl shape? What is the maximum size of nail the bowls would take? Can you design any other method of dispensing small nails?

The real pleasure of craft work comes when you are able to express your feelings and ideas in wood, experimenting, inventing, creating, and finding complete satisfaction in your work. There is no instant method of reaching this happy state. Enthusiasm is not enough. There must also be a knowledge of tools, materials, and processes, a reasonable standard of technical skill, and a keen interest in many other subjects, particularly art, from which you will learn much about colour, form, and design.

Exercises

1. Describe, and illustrate with sketches, any job you have made in school, or any job you would like to make, giving thought to:
   (a) Its function and purpose.
   (b) Appearance
   (c) Construction
   (d) Wood used and finish required.
   (EAST MIDLAND REGIONAL EXAMINATIONS BOARD)

2. Design a portable nail box, suitable for general use, to hold a small quantity of 25 mm, 38 mm, 50 mm, and 100 mm nails.
   (EAST ANGLIAN REGIONAL EXAMINATIONS BOARD)

3. Design a coat-rack, with not more than three pegs, suitable for fixing to the wall. The back-board or frame should not be larger than 500 mm by 150 mm.
   (EAST ANGLIAN REGIONAL EXAMINATIONS BOARD)

4. (a) Provide sketches, showing the design and construction of a picnic table, approximately 750 mm by 450 mm, with folding legs. Add six further main measurements and state the finish you would use.
   (b) Make out a cutting list for this table.
   (c) Print neatly, between two lines, 6 mm apart:
   A FOLDING PICNIC TABLE
   (WELSH JOINT EDUCATION COMMITTEE)

5. Design a table upon which a 533 mm television set is to stand. Include a shelf for the weekly television papers.

6. When designing a cutlery box, what must you first find out before deciding on the final dimensions?
   (SOUTH-EAST REGIONAL EXAMINATIONS BOARD)

145

15
Wood-turning

The wood lathe is used for turning wood to form cylinders, cones, and discs, or any combination of these shapes. Such items include bread boards, teapot stands, fruit bowls, egg cups, tool handles, table lamps, and table legs, Fig. 235.

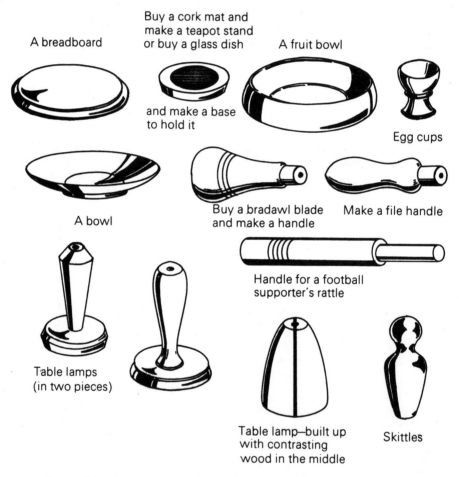

A breadboard

Buy a cork mat and make a teapot stand or buy a glass dish

and make a base to hold it

A fruit bowl

Egg cups

A bowl

Buy a bradawl blade and make a handle

Make a file handle

Handle for a football supporter's rattle

Table lamps (in two pieces)

Table lamp—built up with contrasting wood in the middle

Skittles

Fig. 235a   Some of the objects which can be made on a wood lathe

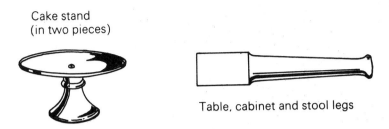

Cake stand
(in two pieces)

Table, cabinet and stool legs

Fig. 235b

Bed. This is made of cast iron and mounted on legs. The bed top is machined straight and flat to provide the ways, shears, or guide rails, Fig. 236.

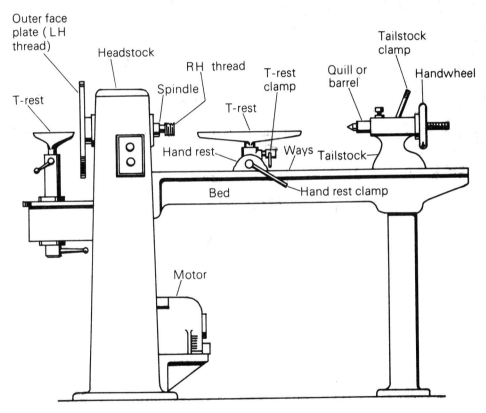

Fig. 236   Wood-turning lathe

Headstock. This is mounted at the left-hand end of the lathe and contains the spindle, pulley cone, and driving belt.

Spindle. This is a hollow shaft which rotates the work, and is mounted in ball bearings. Both ends of the spindle are threaded to take faceplates. The right-hand or inner end has a right-hand thread and the left-hand or outer end has a left-hand thread, so that in use the faceplates tend to tighten on the spindle. The drive is by means of a V-belt, and different speeds are possible by moving the belt to different pairs of pulleys. The largest motor pulley driving the smallest spindle pulley provides the fastest speed. The speeds vary from about 425 to 2250 revolutions per minute (rev/min), but 425 rev/min is suitable for the turning of hardwood bowls and other large diameter work, and 790 rev/min is fast enough for turning smaller work between centres. Higher speeds are only used on very small diameter work and when boring.

Tailstock. A casting mounted at the right-hand end of the lathe and which can be moved along the shears to suit the length of the work. By means of a clamping lever it can be locked to the lathe bed.

Barrel. The hollow spindle mounted in the tailstock; in line with, and exactly opposite to, the spindle. The inside is hollow and shaped to take a centre or drill chuck. The barrel is moved a short distance in or out of the tailstock by means of a handwheel and locked in position.

Hand rest. A cast iron base, lying across the ways and free to move about the lathe bed so that it can be locked in different positions.

T-rest. This fits in the hand rest and can be locked at different heights. The tool must always rest on the T which is supplied in two lengths, 190 mm and 355 mm, to suit different lengths of work.

Fork centre, Fig. 237. Used for holding and driving a length of wood held between centres. It has a centre point and two prongs. Each prong is flat faced on the driving side and chamfered on the back to give a knife edge. It is tapered to fit in the spindle nose.

Cone centre. Used in the tailstock barrel for supporting long lengths of large diameter wood. The 60-degree point acts as a cone-bearing for the work.

Cup centre. A centre used for supporting long lengths of small diameter wood. The nose has a cone-point and is surrounded by a metal rim, both of which enter the wood and support it. The rim reduces the risk of the wood being split by the cone-point.

Screw-flange chuck. A cast iron plate, having a large gauge wood screw in the centre for holding work. The screw is held in place by an Allen screw and can be changed when damaged or broken. This type of chuck should only be used for the turning of small bowls and a better bearing surface is obtained by placing a plywood disc between the work and the faceplate.

Screw-cup chuck. A cast iron plate, screwed to take a clamp ring and used for the holding of short lengths of wood which have to be worked on their ends, as when hollowing egg cups. The wood must be turned to provide a holding flange on one end. The clamp ring passes over this and screws the wood securely to the body of the chuck.

Three-jaw chuck. For convenience, speed, and safety the 3-jaw chuck is very popular for the holding of short lengths of wood. All three jaws move together when the chuck key is turned, so that the chuck is self-centreing and will only hold cylindrical work.

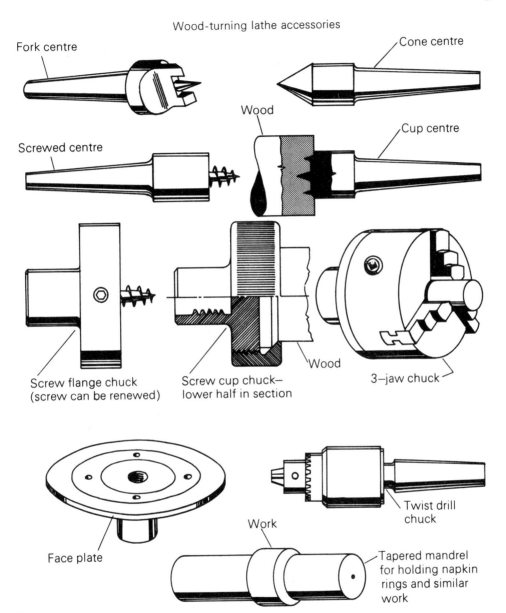

Wood-turning lathe accessories

Fork centre

Cone centre

Screwed centre

Wood

Cup centre

Screw flange chuck
(screw can be renewed)

Screw cup chuck—
lower half in section

Wood

3–jaw chuck

Face plate

Work

Twist drill
chuck

Tapered mandrel
for holding napkin
rings and similar
work

Fig. 237

Faceplates. A circular disc of aluminium or cast iron, having a central screwed boss for fixing to the spindle. Standard equipment consists of a 150 mm inner faceplate and a 300 mm outer faceplate for the holding of blocks of wood up to 450 mm diameter.

Bowls this size are seldom made during a normal course of school work, and if a metal lathe is available the outer faceplate could be reduced to 150 mm diameter for safety and convenience. This size is more suited to the average bowl diameter which rarely exceeds 250 mm.

Faceplates are used when turning bowls and discs such as bread boards and teapot stands, and a number of screw holes countersunk on the back are arranged over the surface so that the work can be held with stout wood screws.

Mandrel. When turning small items having a hole right through, such as napkin rings, the work should be bored to size then pushed on a tapered cylinder of wood known as a mandrel. Chalk rubbed on the mandrel improves the grip. The mandrel is mounted between centres when the work can be turned all over.

Tools, Fig. 238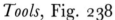

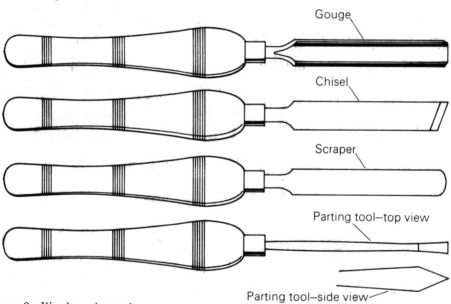

Fig. 238   Wood-turning tools

Turning tools fall into three main groups; gouges, chisels, and scrapers. They have long blades and handles for extra leverage giving better control against the cutting pressure. Because of their size and weight, turning tools should be stored in a rack near the lathe. This prevents them rolling off the lathe and injuring the operator, and also protects the cutting edge.

The tools are made in two strengths, (a) *standard*, and (b) *long and strong*, the latter being more suitable for school use.

GOUGES

These are used for roughing cuts. There are two kinds of curve, *normal* for the heavy turning of cylinders and hollowing between centres, and *deep* for bowl work, Fig. 239.

SKEW CHISELS

These are used for light finishing cuts between centres. The bevel is ground on both sides and with the cutting edge sloping or skewed. This skew is necessary to avoid the top corner of the blade catching in the wood resulting in a severe jolt. The cutting is done with the lower half of the blade to prevent this.

The grinding angle of the gouge and chisel is quite large and is necessary for blade strength, Fig. 240.

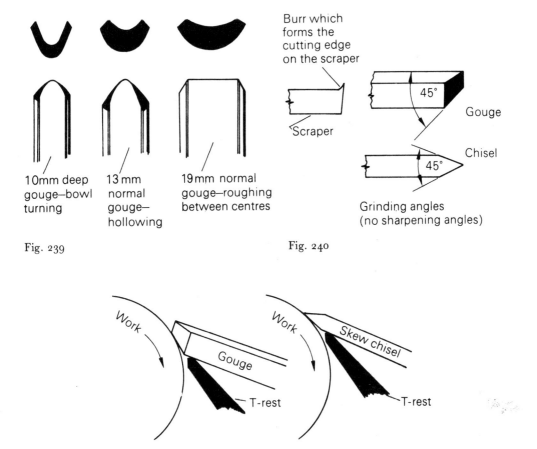

10mm deep gouge—bowl turning

13 mm normal gouge—hollowing

19mm normal gouge—roughing between centres

Fig. 239

Burr which forms the cutting edge on the scraper

Scraper

45° Gouge

Chisel 45°

Grinding angles (no sharpening angles)

Fig. 240

Work

Gouge

T-rest

Work

Skew chisel

T-rest

Fig. 241 Cutting positions. The bevel of the gouge and chisel must rub on the revolving wood. The T-rest must be set for this

In use, it is most important to hold the gouge or chisel so that the bevel rubs on the revolving wood, Fig. 241. Different shapes are formed by moving the gouge on one side or the other and this means that the handle must be moved up, down, or sideways to keep the bevel rubbing on the work.

SCRAPERS

These are used for working in awkward corners, difficult shapes, and finishing hardwood bowls. Several are required to provide a variety of curves. The scraper is sharpened by grinding the end so as to form a burr on the top edge, or the burr can be pressed on with the back of a gouge. In use, the T-rest is withdrawn about 6 mm or more from the work, and the scraper held tilting downwards so that the edge trails, Fig. 242. Never hold a scraper upwards against the revolving work. Use the scraper after the gouge, or where sharp corners and shapes have to be formed.

Avoid too much scraping, not only does this overheat the tool, but it suggests that the gouge should be used.

PARTING OFF TOOL

This chisel has a narrow, straight cutting-edge, slightly wider than the body for blade clearance in the groove. In use, the tool is placed on the T-rest with its bevel resting on the revolving wood, Fig. 243. The handle is gradually raised so that the tool cuts in and down towards the centre of the work.

Care must be taken when ordering turning tools, most of which are too light for work on power driven lathes, and nearly all have small angled bevels which are weak. The following list of turning tools is suggested for most ordinary work, other tools could be added as required.

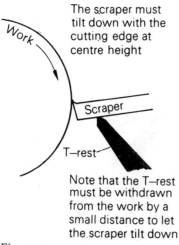

The scraper must tilt down with the cutting edge at centre height

Note that the T-rest must be withdrawn from the work by a small distance to let the scraper tilt down

Fig. 242

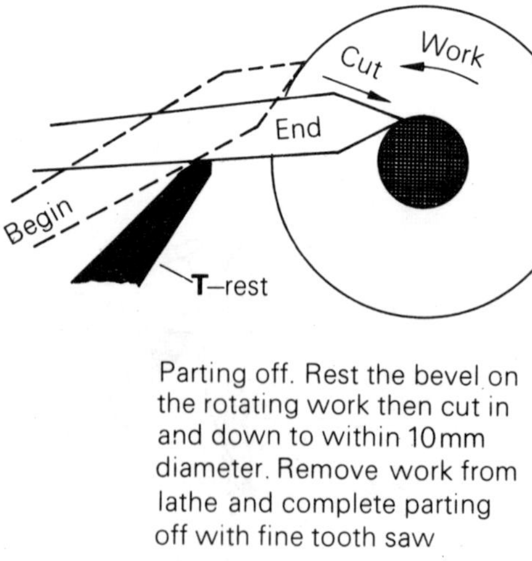

Parting off. Rest the bevel on the rotating work then cut in and down to within 10mm diameter. Remove work from lathe and complete parting off with fine tooth saw

Fig. 243

152

1. For heavy cuts and hollowing on wood between centres:
   Gouges, long and strong, 13 mm and 19 mm.
2. For bowl-turning:
   Gouges, deep curved, long and strong, 10 mm and 13 mm.
3. For finishing cuts on wood between centres:
   Skew chisel, long and strong, 25 mm.
4. For bowl finishing and shaped work:
   Scrapers, long and strong, various shapes, 13 mm to 19 mm.
5. Parting off tool, long and strong.

Turning between Centres, Fig. 244

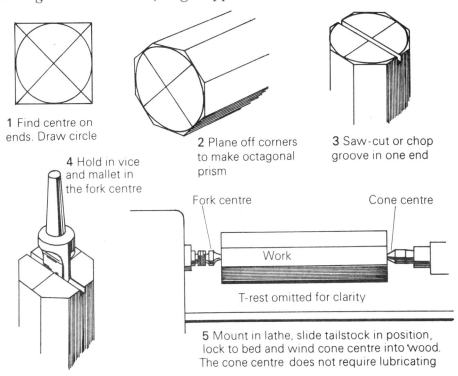

1 Find centre on ends. Draw circle

2 Plane off corners to make octagonal prism

3 Saw-cut or chop groove in one end

4 Hold in vice and mallet in the fork centre

Fork centre

Cone centre

Work

T-rest omitted for clarity

5 Mount in lathe, slide tailstock in position, lock to bed and wind cone centre into wood. The cone centre does not require lubricating

Fig. 244   Turning between centres

The ends of the wood are sawn square and the centres found by drawing diagonals with a pencil and rule. With pencil compasses, draw a circle to touch all four sides then plane off the corners to produce an octagonal section. This shape is smoother and safer to turn because it avoids the danger of the corners banging against the tool. Make a small hole with a bradawl in the centre at each end, and saw right across one end through the

153

centre and about 3 mm deep. Alternatively, a wedge-shaped cut can be made through the centre using a 25 mm chisel and mallet. Hold the work in the vice and drive the fork centre into the middle of the cut. Place the work and fork centre in the lathe, slide the tailstock in position and lock it to the bed. Now turn the handwheel to bring the tail-stock centre into the bradawl hole. Tighten it hard to press both centres well in place, then ease off a little to permit free rotation of the work without slackness. The hand rest

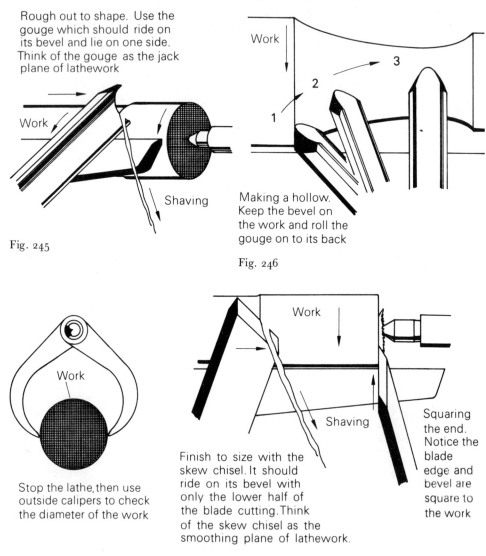

Rough out to shape. Use the gouge which should ride on its bevel and lie on one side. Think of the gouge as the jack plane of lathework

Work

Shaving

Fig. 245

Work

1 2 3

Making a hollow. Keep the bevel on the work and roll the gouge on to its back

Fig. 246

Work

Stop the lathe, then use outside calipers to check the diameter of the work

Fig. 247

Work

Shaving

Finish to size with the skew chisel. It should ride on its bevel with only the lower half of the blade cutting. Think of the skew chisel as the smoothing plane of lathework.

Squaring the end. Notice the blade edge and bevel are square to the work

Fig. 248

154

is locked in position and the T-rest secured just below the centre height. The wood must now be spun round by hand to check that it spins freely.

The lathe is started, a square nosed gouge placed on the T-rest and its bevel brought to bear on the revolving wood when it will cut. By slightly rolling the gouge on its side it can be fed along the wood to remove shavings, Fig. 245. The left hand should be placed over the blade to direct it to the left or right, and the right hand placed round the end of the handle to give up, down, and curved movements to the blade as required. When shaping, work from the larger diameter to the smaller to follow the grain, Fig. 246. Stop the lathe occasionally and check the diameters with calipers, Fig. 247.

For the smooth finishing cut, the T-rest is fixed just above the centre height. With the lathe running, the skew chisel is placed on the T-rest and the bevel gradually brought to rest on the revolving work. With the lower edge of the blade cutting, the chisel is fed along the work to slice off fine shavings, Fig. 248. Because the bevel rubs along the wood the surface of the work should be smooth and shining and require very little glasspapering. The ends of the wood can be trimmed square using the skew chisel on its edge and with the bevel rubbing along the face being cut. Small shapes, such as beads, should be cut in with the skew chisel, and the waste on either side removed with a scraper, Fig. 249.

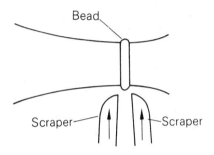

When a bead has to be turned, cut a V-groove on either side then scrape to shape

Fig. 249

Bowl-turning, Fig. 250

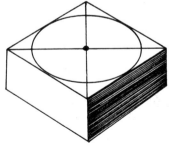

1 Cut block to approximate size. Find centre and mark largest possible circle

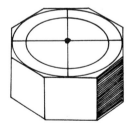

2 Saw off corners to make octagonal prism. Mark guide circle slightly bigger than faceplate

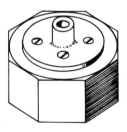

3 Screw on faceplate using No 10 wood screws

Fig. 250   Turning a bowl

Select a suitable block of hardwood, find the centre, and describe the largest possible circle. Using this circle as a guide, saw off as much waste as possible to make the wood fairly circular. Mark a circle on the wood slightly larger than the faceplate and use it as a guide to screw the wood centrally to the faceplate, using three or four No. 10 wood screws. Mount the work on the lathe, set the T-rest close to the face of the wood and a little below the centre height. Turn the outside to shape, using a bowl turning gouge, Fig. 251, then turn the flat base, scraping the central part with a scraper, Fig. 252.

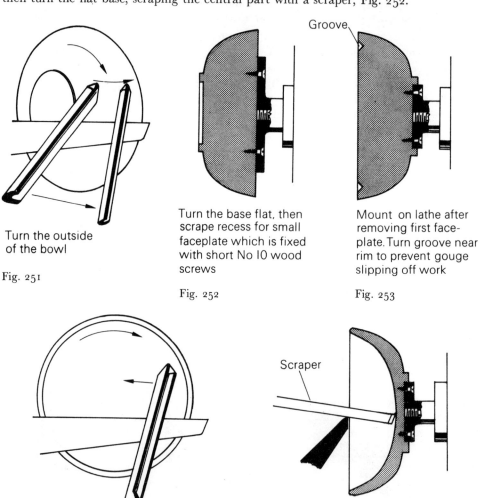

Turn the outside
of the bowl

Fig. 251

Turn the base flat, then
scrape recess for small
faceplate which is fixed
with short No 10 wood
screws

Fig. 252

Groove

Mount on lathe after
removing first face-
plate. Turn groove near
rim to prevent gouge
slipping off work

Fig. 253

Turn inside of bowl using gouge
as much as possible

Fig. 254

Scraper

Finish with scrapers

Fig. 255

To turn the inside means that the bowl must be reversed and the base screwed to the faceplate. There are several ways of doing this, but one of the simplest is to scrape a recess in the base to take another faceplate and screw it in place, Fig. 253.

When turning the inside of the bowl, begin by cutting with the chisel a groove near the rim to prevent the gouge slipping off the work and damaging the edge. The waste is shaved out by keeping the gouge bevel on the wood and scooping it towards the centre, Fig. 254. If bowl-turning on the inner side of the lathe, the bed will interfere with the free movement of the gouge handle and it is for this reason that the outer end has been developed for bowl work. After the bowl has been brought almost to size and the thickness checked, the work can be finished off with scrapers, Fig. 255.

Boring

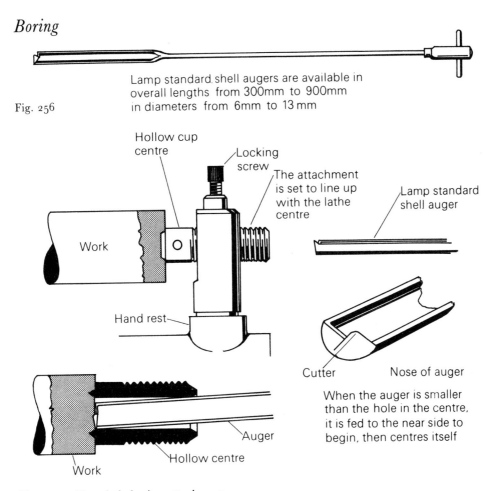

Fig. 256

Lamp standard shell augers are available in overall lengths from 300mm to 900mm in diameters from 6mm to 13 mm

Hollow cup centre

Locking screw

The attachment is set to line up with the lathe centre

Lamp standard shell auger

Work

Hand rest

Cutter   Nose of auger

When the auger is smaller than the hole in the centre, it is fed to the near side to begin, then centres itself

Auger

Hollow centre

Work

Fig. 257a   Deep hole boring attachment

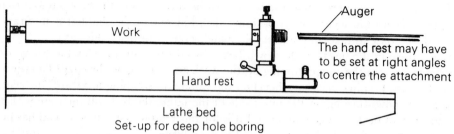

Fig. 257b

Short lengths of wood can be held in a chuck and bored with a twist drill or bit, using a drill chuck in the tailstock. For the boring of long holes in wood held between centres, a lamp standard shell auger is used, Fig. 256. The T-rest is removed and a deep-hole boring attachment mounted in its place, using the tailstock centre as a guide to position it on the centre line, both horizontally and vertically, after which it is locked in position. The tailstock is now removed from the lathe bed and placed on one side out of the way. The hollow centre is screwed into the end of the work using a short tommy bar, then locked in place with a set screw, Fig. 257. The lathe is set to run at 1330 rev/min and the auger fed through the hollow centre. During the boring operation, remove the auger after every 50 or 75 mm to remove the waste wood. The hole diameter in the hollow centre should suit the size of the auger and an 8 mm hole is suitable for the ever-popular table lamps.

Glasspapering

If the tools have been used correctly, that is with their bevels riding on the revolving work so that shavings are cut, only a brief rub with glasspaper will be required to finish. Begin with No. 1 and finish with No. 0, holding the paper under the wood as it revolves and completing the operation in a few minutes. Stop the lathe, and, using the same glasspaper, rub the wood along the grain to remove any remaining marks. Finally, run the lathe and press a handful of shavings against the underside of the wood to polish it by friction. The wood should now shine and is ready for the finishing treatment.

Exercises

1. State the purpose of each of the following:
   (a) T-rest; (b) tailstock; (c) fork centre; (d) cone centre; (e) cup centre.

2. (a) For what kind of turning would you use a square-edge gouge?
   (b) At what position would you fix the T-rest?
   (c) Make a neat sketch to show the grinding angle of the gouge.

3. (a) For what kind of turning would you use a skew chisel?

(b) Why is the blade skewed?

(c) At what position would you fix the T-rest?

4. Describe one method of reversing a bowl after turning the base so that the inside can be turned.

5. Assume that you have just finished turning a bowl from hardwood and that it is intended to use it as a salad bowl. Give an account of the steps you would take to finish the bowl ready for use.

(MIDDLESEX REGIONAL EXAMINING BOARD)

6. You are required to make a bowl on the lathe from a piece of hardwood measuring 250 mm × 250 mm × 75 mm. Make a series of notes and sketches showing the work you will do.

Use the following sub-titles:

(a) Preparation of wood before mounting.

(b) Mounting the wood and setting up the lathe.

(c) Cutting tools in action for the outside.

(d) Reversing the bowl.

(e) Cutting tools in action for the inside.

(f) Cleaning up and polishing.

Your sketches should include one showing a cross-section of the bowl.

(SOUTH-EAST REGIONAL EXAMINATIONS BOARD)

7. If you were intending to turn the column of a table lamp on the lathe, from a piece of wood 50 mm square and 300 mm long, explain how you would:

(a) prepare the wood for the lathe;

(b) set up the wood in the lathe;

(c) turn it to shape.

(SOUTHERN REGIONAL EXAMINATIONS BOARD)

8. Name four safety precautions which should be observed before and whilst using a wood-worker's lathe.

(WELSH JOINT EDUCATION COMMITTEE)

16

Timbers

The following notes on some of the more popular timbers are intended as a guide only. For them to be of real value, you should also examine actual specimens of each kind of timber, make notes of your own, and learn to identify each. Notice the smell, especially when the wood is freshly sawn, and test its weight. Chestnut and oak look very similar, but oak is much heavier. Examine the end grain, and compare the faces of the wood when plain and quarter sawn. The usefulness of different kinds of timber varies and qualities such as strength, colour, durability, and ease of working are known as their characteristics. Because they vary considerably in different kinds of timber it is important that you should be able to identify and know something of the timbers available to you.

In classifying the durability of timber, the Forest Products Research Laboratory uses five grades as follows:

GRADE OF DURABILITY	APPROXIMATE LIFE IN CONTACT WITH THE GROUND (YEARS)
Very durable	More than 25
Durable	15–25
Moderately durable	10–15
Non-durable	5–10
Perishable	Less than 5

All the following timbers can be glued, nailed, screwed, stained, polished and painted, unless otherwise stated.

Softwoods

DOUGLAS FIR,

known as *Colombian pine* in Great Britain.

Grown on the western side of Canada and the U.S.A., and now grown in Europe, New Zealand, and Australia. The timber has a brown heartwood and pale coloured sapwood. There is a strong contrast between the springwood and the summerwood resulting in 'blister' figure on rotary cut veneers. The wood is usually straight-grained, slightly resinous, strong, and moderately durable. It works well, but care is required when nailing to prevent splitting.

Uses. More plywood is produced from Douglas Fir than any other timber. Being strong it is used for heavy construction work as well as roofing, joinery, vats and tanks for chemical plants and breweries, and paper pulp.

PARANA PINE

Grown in South America.

The timber has a light brown coloured heartwood, often with red streaks, and a pale coloured sapwood. The grain is usually straight, but the growth rings are not easily seen. Although the wood is strong it lacks toughness and should not be used for the sides of ladders. It is non-durable, and works easily and well, resulting in a smooth finish.

Uses. In South America it is used for plywood manufacture and joinery, and is to the South Americans what the Scots Pine is to Europeans. In Great Britain it is used for bus building, joinery, and interior work not exposed to the weather.

SCOTS PINE,

also known as *redwood, red deal* (in northern England), *yellow deal* (southern England), fir, and many other names.

Grown all over Europe.

The timber varies because of its wide distribution. The heartwood is pale reddish brown and the sapwood light coloured. Sometimes the wood is marked with a blue stain caused by a harmless fungus. The wood is non-durable and works quite well, though knots may be troublesome.

Uses. Constructional work of all kinds, joinery, carpentry, turnery, lorries, railway work, pit props, and paper pulp.

SITKA SPRUCE,

or *silver spruce.*

Grown along the western coast of North America and Canada.

The timber is a high class lightweight softwood, being non-resinous, odourless, and non-tainting. The heartwood is a light pinkish brown and the sapwood slightly paler coloured. It is non-durable, works well to a good finish, and has good strength for its weight.

Uses. Aeroplane and glider construction, oars, boat building, and the soundboards of pianos.

Hardwoods

ASH, European.

Grown in Europe, North Africa, and western Asia.

The timber is white to pale brown in colour, turning pink when freshly cut. The sapwood and heartwood are the same colour. It is straight-grained and ring porous, resulting in a decorative veneer of value. The wood is strong and tough, has excellent steam bending properties, but is perishable.

Uses. Plywood and veneers for sports goods. Its qualities of bending, toughness, and flexibility make it one of the best woods for sports items such as tennis rackets, hockey sticks, diving boards, and gymnasium equipment. It is also widely used for tool handles, agricultural equipment, lorry frames, wagon and coach building, and curved parts for furniture.

BEECH, European.

Grown in Europe.

The timber is pale brown, but darkens in time to a reddish brown colour. There is seldom any difference between the colour of the sapwood and the heartwood. The wood has a fine even texture with a straight grain, and when quartered the rays show as small flecks all over the surface. It is one of the strongest of the home grown timbers, very good for steam bending, but perishable. Works fairly well, but tends to be tough.

Uses. Plywood, furniture, cabinet making, turnery, tool handles, shoe heels, toys, bobbins, domestic woodware, brush ware, and clog soles. In the United Kingdom, beech is the hardwood used in the largest quantities.

MAHOGANY, African.

Grows in the rain forests of East and West Africa and named after the port from which it is shipped.

The timber has a pink to light brown heartwood with a yellow-brown coloured sapwood. Gum veins spoil the wood. It is fairly straight-grained, but there is some interlocking which produces stripe or roe figure when the timber is quarter sawn. The texture is coarse and grain fractures are a common defect. It is moderately durable and works fairly easily though the hardness varies.

Uses. High class plywood, furniture, joinery, panelling, interior work of all kinds, and boat planking.

MAKORE,

also known as *cherry mahogany*.

Grown in West Africa.

The timber resembles mahogany. The heartwood varies from a pinkish purple brown to a dark blood red with a light coloured sapwood. It has a plain appearance when slash sawn, but shows a mottled figure when quarter sawn. The wood is very durable, heavier than African mahogany, works fairly well, but rapidly blunts the tools, especially saws, and tends to split when nailed. When working with this timber the fine wood dust may irritate the nose and throat.

Uses. High grade plywood, furniture, good class decorative work, veneers, superior joinery, interior fittings, the framework for motor vehicles, laboratory benches, exterior doors, textile rollers, and turnery.

OAK, European.

Grown in southern Europe, southern Asia, and North Africa.

The timber has a yellowish brown heartwood and a pale coloured narrow band of sapwood. The wood shows an attractive silver grain or figure when quarter sawn. The weight and characteristics vary considerably, depending on where the wood was grown and whether growth was fast or slow. The wood contains tannin which causes a blue stain when in contact with iron and steel fittings. Only brass or stainless steel screws should be used in oak because the acid nature of the wood rapidly corrodes iron and steel. It is durable, works well, though can be tough and difficult and should be nailed and screwed with care to avoid splitting.

Uses. Decorative veneers and plywood manufacture. Railway wagon construction, window sills, cart and lorry frames, ladder rungs, posts and rails for fixing in the ground and exposed to the weather. Docks and ship repair work, important parts of ship-building such as stems, stern posts, knee beams, keel, ribs, gunwales, and rudders. The bark is used for the tanning of leather. Brown oak is so coloured because of fungi. It is valued for decorative work, panelling, and joinery.

JAPANESE OAK

This is yellowish brown and of slow, even growth. It is mild and easy to work and has excellent steam bending properties. Its use is mainly for furniture, cabinet work, joinery, and panelling.

SAPELE

Grown in the rain forests from West to East Africa.

The timber has a dark reddish or purplish brown heartwood and a pale coloured sapwood. It is a mahogany and has a very attractive stripe or roe figure when quarter sawn. The texture is fairly fine, but the timber is liable to ring shakes. Moderately durable, and works fairly easily, though interlocked grain can be troublesome.

Uses. Plywood and decorative veneers. Furniture, joinery, shop fittings, flooring, dance floors, and decorative floor blocks.

TEAK

Grown in India, Burma, and Java.

The timber has a golden brown colour with some dark markings. Teak is an outstanding timber because of its many valuable properties. It is strong, durable, of moderate weight, resistant to fire and acids, and does not corrode iron and steel fittings.

The wood is straight-grained and works well, but the gritty nature of the wood dulls cutting tools. It tends to be brittle and care is needed when nailing. Teak has a greasy feel due to the presence of oil which may cause some difficulty when gluing. This can be overcome by degreasing the actual joint area or using a synthetic resin glue.

Uses. Plywood and decorative veneers. Important for shipbuilding, including deck planks, deck houses, rails, hatches, weather doors, furniture and interior fittings of boats. Constructional work such as doors and window frames, indoor and garden furniture, vats and fittings in chemical plants, especially laboratory bench tops.

WALNUT, American,

also known as *black walnut.*
Grown on the eastern side of the U.S.A. and Canada.

The timber has a rich brown heartwood with an occasional purplish tinge and a pale coloured sapwood. The wood is hard, heavy, and usually straight-grained, though attractively figured wood is often found. The texture is fine and smooth. It works well and takes an excellent finish.

Uses. Decorative veeneers, high class furniture and cabinet work, rifle and gun stocks, and aeroplane propellers.

WALNUT, European.

Grown in Europe and Asia.

The timber has a greyish brown heartwood marked with irregular dark streaks which gives it an attractive appearance. The sapwood is pale coloured. The wood is moderately durable, fairly hard but easy to work. It finishes well and takes an excellent polish. Because it cuts cleanly, it is suitable for carved work. Attractively figured veneers are available from burrs, crotches, and stumps.

Uses. Decorative veneers, fancy goods such as turned fruit bowls, high class cabinet work, and rifle and gun stocks because of its resistance to shock.

Exercises

1. Make a chart to show the characteristics of the following timbers:
   Softwoods: Larch, western red cedar, yellow pine.
   Hardwoods: Abura, afrormosia, agba, chestnut, elm, jelutong, Honduras mahogany, rauli, sycamore, utile.

2. Write brief notes on: ebony, balsa, and rosewood.
   State clearly, and with reasons, the special use of each.

3. Name four different timbers used for making woodworkers' tools and equipment, saying for what purposes they are used and giving reasons for using them.
   (WEST MIDLANDS EXAMINATIONS BOARD)

4. What timbers are most likely to be used for the following:
   (a) a hammer shaft, (b) a wooden jack plane, (c) the stock of a try square?

   (SOUTH-EAST REGIONAL EXAMINATIONS BOARD)

5. What timber would you use for making:
   (a) a garden shed; (b) a garden fence; (c) a pair of household steps; (d) a tea trolley; (e) a model glider; (f) the handle of a firmer chisel?
   Give reasons for your choice.

Glossary

This has been adapted from the fuller and more detailed B.S. 565:1963, *Glossary of Terms Relating to Timber and Woodwork*. Where a choice of terms appears, that appearing first is favoured with the alternative following. Terms disapproved because of confusion, appear in brackets.

ARRIS. A sharp edge of wood. If the sharpness is removed it is known as an eased arris.

CLAMP. A strip of wood fixed across the grain of timber to prevent warping.

CHECK. A small crack along the grain not extending from one surface to the other. It usually occurs during seasoning.

CLEAN. Timber which is free from knots.

CLEAR. Timber which is free from visible defects.

DEAD (not bare). Exact size.

EDGE. (i) The narrow side of square sawn timber.
      (ii) To remove the wane by sawing.

END. The cross-cut surface of square sawn timber.

FACE. The broad side of square sawn timber.

FIGURE. Ornamental markings, seen on the cut surface of timber, formed by the structure of the wood.

FILLET. A narrow strip of wood.

FULL. Oversize.

GRAIN. The general direction or arrangement of the fibres.

HARDWOOD. The timber of broad-leaved trees.

HEART. The portion of a log which includes the pith and the surrounding defective wood.
    Note: Not to be confused with heartwood.

HEARTWOOD. Wood which in the growing tree had ceased to contain living cells.

KERF. A saw cut.

KNOT. A portion of a branch enclosed in the wood by the natural growth of the tree.

LEDGE, BEARER, CLEAT. A member nailed across a number of boards to hold them together in carpentry.

LEDGE. An unframed piece of wood used for the purpose of stiffening or holding together a board or series of boards in joinery.

MOISTURE CONTENT. The amount of moisture in timber or other material expressed as a percentage of its oven-dry weight.

166

MORTICE. A hole or slot to receive a tenon.

MORTISE. To cut a mortice in.

MOULDING. (i) A shape cut upon wood for ornament.

            (ii) A moulded piece of wood.

PITH, HEART CENTRE. The central core of a stem.

PLAIN SAWN, FLAT GRAIN, FLAT-SAWN, SLASH GRAIN TIMBER. Timber converted so that the growth rings meet the face at an angle of less than 45 degrees.

QUARTER SAWN, RIFT-SAWN, EDGE GRAIN, VERTICAL GRAIN, COMB GRAIN, QUARTERED TIMBER. Timber converted so that the growth rings meet the face at an angle of not less than 45 degrees.

RAY, MEDULLARY RAY, PITH RAY, WOOD RAY. A strip or ribbon of tissue extending radially in the stem.

RAIL. A horizontal piece of wood in a frame.

SAPWOOD. The outer layers of wood which in the growing tree contained living cells.

SCANT (not bare). Undersize.

SEASONING, DRYING. The process of drying timber for use.

SHAKE. A large crack along the grain which may develop in the standing tree, or in felling or in seasoning.

SOFTWOOD. The timber of coniferous trees.

SPLIT. A crack along the grain extending through the wood from one surface to another.

SPRINGWOOD, EARLY WOOD. The less dense wood formed during the earlier stages of the growth of each annual ring.

STILE. A vertical piece of wood in a frame.

SUMMERWOOD (not autumn wood). The denser wood formed during the later stages of growth of each annual ring.

TEXTURE. The structural character of wood as revealed by touch or reaction to cutting tools. Common descriptive terms are as follows:

Coarse texture: large elements or unusually wide growth rings.

Even texture: little variation in the size of its elements or little contrast between springwood and summerwood.

Fine texture (not close texture): small elements or narrow growth rings.

Uneven texture: having considerable variation in the size of the elements and with a distinct contrast between springwood and summerwood.

Book list

LAIC, L. H. and JONES, D. A. *Designing in Wood*, Harrap, 1968.

HAYNES, F. A. *Learning Woodwork*, Pergamon, 1966.

GLENISTER, S. H. *Contemporary Design in Woodwork*, Vols. 1 and 2, Murray, 1968.

BAYNES, K. *Industrial Design and the Community*, Lund Humphries, 1967.

A Handbook of Hardwoods } Department of Scientific and Industrial Research, Forest
A Handbook of Softwoods } Products Research, H.M.S.O.

Woodwork Chisels and Gouges, B.S. 1943:1953.

Glossary of Terms Relating to Timber and Woodwork, B.S. 565:1963, British Standards
Institution.

Index

Index